KONVENS 2024 - GermEval 2024 Task 1 GermsMS-Detect

Proceedings of the GermEval 2024 Task 1 GerMS-Detect Workshop on Sexism Detection in German Online News Fora (GerMS-Detect 2024)

Vienna, Austria
10 September 2024

ISBN: 979-8-3313-0485-0

Printed from e-media with permission by:

Curran Associates, Inc.
57 Morehouse Lane
Red Hook, NY 12571

CURRAN ASSOCIATES INC.
proceedings.com

Some format issues inherent in the e-media version may also appear in this print version.

Association for Computational Linguistics
209 N. Eighth Street
Stroudsburg, Pennsylvania 18360

Phone: 1-570-476-8006
Fax: 1-570-476-0860

acl@aclweb.org

Additional copies of this publication are available from:

Curran Associates, Inc.
57 Morehouse Lane
Red Hook, NY 12571 USA
Phone: 845-758-0400
Fax: 845-758-2633
Email: curran@proceedings.com
Web: www.proceedings.com

GerMS-Detect 2024

KONVENS 2024 – GermEval 2024 Task 1 GerMS-Detect

Proceedings of the GermEval 2024 Task 1 GerMS-Detect Workshop on Sexism Detection in German Online News Fora

September 10, 2024

The GerMS-Detect organizers gratefully acknowledge the support from the following sponsors.

Supported by

Austrian Research Institute for Artificial Intelligence

asai austrian society for artificial intelligence

Federal Ministry Republic of Austria Climate Action, Environment, Energy, Mobility, Innovation and Technology

Order copies of this and other ACL proceedings from:

Association for Computational Linguistics (ACL)
317 Sidney Baker St. S
Suite 400 - 134
Kerrville, TX 78028
USA
Tel: +1-855-225-1962
acl@aclweb.org

Table of Contents

GermEval2024 Shared Task: GerMS-Detect – Sexism Detection in German Online News Fora
Stephanie Gross, Johann Petrak, Louisa Venhoff and Brigitte Krenn 1

THAugs at GermEval 2024 (Shared Task 1: GerMS-Detect): Predicting the Severity of Misogyny/Sexism in Forum Comments with BERT Models (Subtask 1, Closed Track and Additional Experiments)
Cosin Geiss and Alessandra Zarcone 10

FICODE at GermEval 2024 GerMS-Detect closed ST1 & ST2: Ensemble- and Transformer-Based Detection of Sexism and Misogyny in German Texts
Maoro Falk and Michaela Geierhos 21

Team Quabynar at the GermEval 2024 Shared Task 1 GerMS-Detect (Subtasks 1 and 2) on Sexism Detection
Kwabena Odame Akomeah, Udo Kruschwitz and Bernd Ludwig 26

Detecting Sexism in German Online Newspaper Comments with Open-Source Text Embeddings (Team GDA, GermEval2024 Shared Task 1: GerMS-Detect, Subtasks 1 and 2, Closed Track)
Florian Bremm, Patrick Gustav Blaneck, Tobias Bornheim, Niklas Grieger and Stephan Bialonski 33

pd2904 at GermEval2024 (Shared Task 1: GerMS-Detect): Exploring the Effectiveness of Multi-Task Transformers vs. Traditional Models for Sexism Detection (Closed Tracks of Subtasks 1 and 2)
Pia Donabauer 39

GermEval2024 Shared Task: GerMS-Detect – Sexism Detection in German Online News Fora

Stephanie Gross, Johann Petrak, Louisa Venhoff, Brigitte Krenn
Austrian Research Institute for Artificial Intelligence (OFAI)
Freyung 6/6, 1010 Vienna, Austria
firstname.lastname@ofai.at

Abstract

We present an overview of the GermEval2024 shared task: GerMS-Detect on the detection of sexism and misogyny in the German language comments of online news fora. The data were annotated by a varying number of human annotators with regard to whether or not the comment is sexist or misogynist in a way that could discourage women from participating in the discussion. Ambiguous comments or comments which may contain more subtle forms of misogyny have often been judged and annotated differently by the human annotators. For this task, rather than assuming the existence of one "true" label for each comment, we accept that judgements on the presence or strength of misogyny can be highly subjective and encourage the development of models which can be used to reflect the potential disagreement for some of the comments. For this reason, the shared task was divided into two subtasks, where subtask 1 focused on classification models capable of detecting binary or ordinal levels of misogyny derived in different ways from the labels provided by the human annotators as well on predicting whether or not there is disagreement between the annotators of the comment. Subtask 2 was concerned with directly approximating the distribution of labels a group of specific annotators is likely to assign to a specific comment. Seven teams participated in subtask 1 and six participated in subtask 2. Of these, five teams contributed a paper for the workshop.

Content warning: We show illustrative examples of sexist and misogynous language.

1 Introduction and Motivation

Sexist and misogynist comments in online social media or other online fora can be harmful and be an important factor why women refrain from participating in online discussions. This effect of silencing women in online fora may get caused also by comments with subtle or implicit forms of misogyny. This calls for the deployment of tools to identify sexist content to support content moderation and monitoring. However, identifying sexist content is also a challenging task for humans because they often refer to some implied context which is not available or is formulated in a subtle way, avoiding strong or outright offensive language. Therefore the manually annotated datasets on which classifiers are trained on potentially contain high human annotator variation for the same content. The up to date prevalent approach is to unify diverging annotator opinions, assuming a ground truth, e.g., by employing majority vote, subsequent consensus by the annotators, or a decision by a meta reviewer. Plank (2022) emphasizes that human label variation needs more attention in machine learning research, as it impacts data, modeling and the evaluation of machine learning systems. Although the interest in preserving annotator variation is increasing (e.g., Pavlick and Kwiatkowski, 2019; Uma et al., 2021b; Plank, 2022; Davani et al., 2022), and relevant workshops and shared tasks were already organized in recent years (e.g., Abercrombie et al., 2022; Uma et al., 2021a; Ojha et al., 2023), multi-perspective approaches are still in their infancy.

We organized the GermEval2024 Shared Task: GerMS-Detect – Sexism Detection in German Online News Fora, with the goal to contribute to this line of research. This shared task also follows from success of previous shared tasks on sexism detection (such as Fersini et al., 2018; Basile et al., 2019; Kirk et al., 2023).

The corpus used in this shared task was collected from comments in the fora of a large Austrian online news site (derStandard.at[1]). The annotations reflect the newspaper's forum moderation policy regarding sexism and misogyny. Moreover, the definition of sexism reflected in the annotation guide-

[1] https://www.derstandard.at

lines is based on the definition given in Encyclopedia Britannica which defines **sexism** as "prejudice or discrimination based on sex or gender, especially against women and girls", and **misogyny** as "the extreme form of sexist ideology" which they state is "the hatred of women".[2] The corpus was then annotated by multiple annotators with labels ranging from 0 (no sexism/misogyny) over 1 (slight) to 4 (extreme sexism). Annotator judgements tend to differ, especially when the comment lacks context, or is worded in a subtle or deliberately ambiguous way. The goal of the shared task was to explore how different opinions from different annotators can be utilized and reflected in models trained on this corpus, rather than assuming that one label is the correct one to reflect the "true" sexism present in the comment and considering diverging labels as mistakes or noise. See Table 1 for sample *sexist* comments in the data.

Sample:	"Ich mag keine Kampflesben, die sollte man mal allesamt wegsperren"
EN:	"I do not like combat lesbians, they should all be locked away"
Sample:	"Bei aller Tragik und Ernsthaftigkeit.... wir haben schon a fesche Justizministerin"
EN:	"With all tragedy and seriousness.... we definitely have a dashing Minister of Justice"

Table 1: Sample comments from the dataset.

The datasets provided in the shared task contain, in the training set, the individual annotations from each annotator (identified by an annonymized annotator id) and, in the test set, the list of annotators (but not their labels) for which the trained models have to make predictions. The shared task is divided into two subtasks: in subtask 1, binarized and multi-class labels derived from the individual annotator-assigned labels as well as an indicator of annotator disagreement on the presence of sexism are derived from the set of annotations and have to be predicted by the model for the test set. In subtask 2, the distribution of binarized and multi-class labels for the given set of annotators has to be predicted by the model. For both subtasks there was a closed and an open track, where the closed track required that no additional training data or pretrained models which may have been trained for sexism or misogyny detection was allowed and all contributions had to be open source. For the open track, any approach, including proprietary data or models, including large language models, was allowed.

Characteristics which make our shared task unique are: The dataset (i) is in German language, (ii) it includes a high number of expert labels, (iii) it was collected with the goal to provide a more welcoming and safer climate of discussion in online newspaper fora, especially for female users, and (iv) it allows for experimenting with classifier training based on hard and soft labels. Uma et al. (2021b), for example, has shown that with datasets annotated by a high number of expert coders, training directly with soft labels achieved better results than training from aggregated or gold labels.

2 Dataset

Data collection The data stem from fora of a large Austrian online newspaper in German language and consist of 7984 user comments on newspaper articles.[3] They include (i) selected comments which were reported as problematic by forum users, (ii) randomly sampled comments, (iii) comments pre-classified as potentially sexist by a sexism classifier trained on an early subset of the annotated data, and (iv) comments from 24 article fora which were manually identified by forum moderators to contain an above-average number of comments considered as *sexist*. (For more details, see Krenn et al., 2024). The length of the comments ranges from one to 173 words, with a mean of 32 words per comment. The original newline and whitespace characters were preserved.

Data preprocessing For anonymization, (i) URLs were replaced with the placeholder `{URL}`, (ii) At-mentions (e.g. `@name`) were replaced with `{USER}`, (iii) comments were scanned for email addresses, but none were present in the texts, and (iv) each comment was manually checked for potential mentions of user names or nick names by three annotators and systematically replaced with the placeholder `{USER}`.

Further means for privacy protection were that all information indicating the position of a comment within a certain thread was excluded, as well as all information which would allow a comment to

[2]Source: https://www.britannica.com/topic/sexism (Accessed: 2024-07-30). As the dataset employed in the shared task comprises comments which are either sexist or misogynist or both, we use *sexism* or *sexist* to refer to sexist or misogynous comments in this paper.

[3]After the end of the shared task competition phase, all data was made publicly available, see https://huggingface.co/datasets/ofai/GerMS-AT and https://ofai.github.io/GermEval2024-GerMS/download.html.

be associated with a particular article forum. These privacy detection means influences the annotation process, as there is no further context available but only the individual comment text when annotators decide whether a comment is *sexist* or not and to what extent.

Data annotation Goal of the corpus annotation was to learn from moderator judgements in their everyday work. Therefore the majority of annotators who manually labelled the comments were experienced forum moderators (7 out of 10). However, the other three annotators were experienced in corpus annotation. There were 3 annotators who self-identified as male, 7 who self-identified as female, and all annotators were native speakers of German.

The annotators were provided with detailed annotation guidelines including a list of criteria determining what should be classified as *sexist*, covering the newspaper's gender policy. The criteria to judge a comment as sexist referred to in the annotation guidelines are:

- Generalizing stereotypes, i.e., attributions to groups of women, including role stereotypes (e.g., women are better suited for housework) and attribute stereotypes (e.g., women can not think logically)
- Reduction of a person to her appearance
- Women as sexual objects
- Female connoted insult
- Denigration of women, their performance and women's issues, e.g., denial of the existence of gender differences in salary
- Downplay of sexual violence and sexual harassment against women
- Whataboutism, e.g., claiming that men are much more likely to be affected by violence
- Abortion, e.g., abortion is equated with murder
- Misandry: Given a *sexist* utterance against men, can the male referent be replaced by a female referent and does the resulting utterance fall under one of the above categories?

For more details on the annotation guidelines, see (Krenn et al., 2024).

In addition, the annotators were asked to label those comments they have classified as *sexist* on a scale from 1 to 4 according to their personal perception of the severity of sexism expressed in the comment ("How uncomfortable do I feel reading this comment?"). While Röttger et al. (2022) argue to follow either a descriptive or prescriptive annotation paradigm when annotating a dataset, we aimed for a combination of detailed guidelines on what should be considered as sexist (prescriptive paradigm) and the subjective assessment of how sexist a user comment is (descriptive paradigm). This allowed us to create a dataset which captures gradations in the assessment of sexist utterances with twofold use: (i) for the training of binary classifiers (*sexist* versus *non-sexist*); (ii) in machine learning research for how to make models aware of more or less disagreement on labels (e.g., Uma et al., 2021b; Plank, 2022). These two use-cases are reflected in subtask 1 and subtask 2 of the GermEval2024 Shared Task GerMS-Detect, respectively.

Comments were annotated by assigning one of 5 possible labels ($0 - 4$), where 0 is the absence of *sexism* and $1 - 4$ express the levels of subjective severity of the expressed *sexism* as perceived by the individual annotators (1 = mild, 2 = present, 3 = strong, 4 = extreme). Each comment was annotated by 3–10 individual annotators (3 labels: 325 comments, 4 labels: 1073 comments, 5 labels: 6481 comments, 7 labels: 6 comments, 10 labels: 999 comments).

Annotator Agreement and Corpus Analysis Krippendorff Alpha over all annotations was 0.64 (ordinal scale), and for the binary data (sexist vs. not sexist) it was 0.59. According to Hayes and Krippendorff (2007), values over 0.667 are considered to be good. The lower values in the present dataset might be due to the highly subjective nature of what is considered sexist and the assessment of its severity. A Shapiro-Wilk Test showed significant results for all annotators ($p < 0.001$) indicating that the data are not normally distributed. Therefore a Kruskal Wallis H Test was calculated to check for overall significant differences between the means of the annotators. This test was significant with $H = 477.04$, $p < 0.001$. A Dunn-Bonferroni post-hoc test was conducted to compare the individual annotators. This test revealed significant differences ($p <= 0.05$), see Figure 1.

	A001	A002	A003	A004	A005	A007	A008	A009	A010	A012
A001	1.000	0.001	0.353	1.000	1.000	1.000	0.102	0.024	1.000	1.000
A002	0.001	1.000	0.000	0.000	0.000	0.000	1.000	1.000	0.000	0.000
A003	0.353	0.000	1.000	0.039	0.029	0.136	0.000	0.000	0.000	0.000
A004	1.000	0.000	0.039	1.000	1.000	1.000	0.124	0.022	1.000	1.000
A005	1.000	0.000	0.029	1.000	1.000	1.000	0.097	0.014	1.000	1.000
A007	1.000	0.000	0.136	1.000	1.000	1.000	0.062	0.010	1.000	1.000
A008	0.102	1.000	0.000	0.124	0.097	0.062	1.000	1.000	0.806	0.019
A009	0.024	1.000	0.000	0.022	0.014	0.010	1.000	1.000	0.083	0.000
A010	1.000	0.000	0.000	1.000	1.000	1.000	0.806	0.083	1.000	1.000
A012	1.000	0.000	0.000	1.000	1.000	1.000	0.019	0.000	1.000	1.000

Figure 1: Results of a Dunn-Bonferroni post-hoc test comparing individual annotators. Significant differences ($p <= 0.05$) are marked in red.

These low p-values might be due to different reasons:

- Systematic Differences: Individuals may have a systematic difference in how they rate items. For example, one rater consistently gives higher or lower ratings than the other one.
- Rating Bias: One or both raters might have a bias in their ratings, such as always rating items on the higher or lower end of the scale, leading to a significant difference when compared to other raters.
- Consistency in Rating: If one rater is very consistent in their ratings (e.g., always giving the same rating for similar items) while another rater is less consistent or varies more in their ratings, this can lead to significant differences in the distribution of ratings.
- Sample Size: If the number of items rated by each rater is large, even small differences in the average ratings can become statistically significant, leading to very low p-values.
- Scale of Measurement: The scale of ratings (0-4) might accentuate differences, especially if the differences between raters are consistent across many items.

Figure 2 shows the number of items rated by each annotator and their respective ratings. While three annotators labelled 95% of the data or more, the other 7 labelled 16–49%. Also, differences in the subjective assessment of the severity of a user comment are visible. Figure 3 shows the means and distributions of the ratings per annotator.

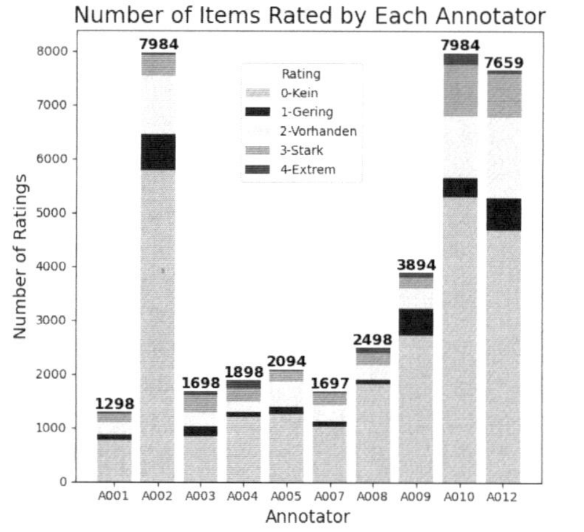

Figure 2: Number of items rated by each of the 10 individual annotators.

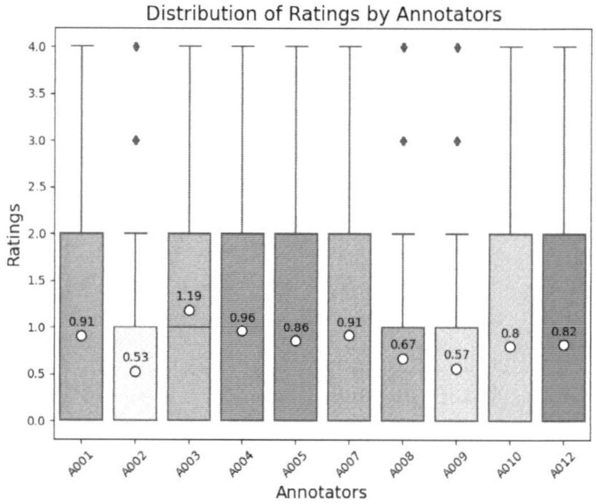

Figure 3: Annotator distributions and means of annotator ratings.

When comparing the significant pairs in the Dunn's test with the plots it becomes clear why some pairs are more significant than others, depending on the amount they rated, their inconsistencies in ratings and their differing means and distributions.

The higher level of subjectivity and the inconsistent number of labels per comment raise challenges for subtask 1 and subtask 2. However, dealing with annotator variation due to subjective assessment and developing robust models based on the dataset with certain inconsistencies are topics we wanted to target in the shared task.

In order to gain more insight in annotator variation, we propose a qualitative analysis of comments with significant disagreement (e.g., a deviation of 3 * the standard deviation), such as qualitative content analysis and inductive category development (see Mayring, 2014). In the dataset discussed in this paper, for example irony, sexism against men, and non-sexist insults might play a role in comments with significant disagreement. However, this is ongoing work and needs further investigation. Additionally, deductive category application might be useful for further analysing significant disagreement in these types of dataset, e.g. the categories proposed by Sandri et al. (2023).

3 Task Description

3.1 Task Definition and Evaluation Metrics

Subtask 1: Classification In subtask 1 the goal was to predict labels for each text in a dataset where the labels are derived from the original labels assigned by several human annotators in several different ways:

- `bin_maj`: predict 1 if a majority of annotators assigned a label other than 0, predict 0 if a majority of annotators assigned a label 0. If there was no majority, then both the label 1 and 0 will count as correct in the evaluation.
- `bin_one`: predict 1 if at least one annotator assigned a label other than 0, 0 otherwise.
- `bin_all`: predict 1 if all annotators assigned labels other than 0, predict 0 otherwise.
- `multi_maj`: predict the majority label if there is one, if there is no majority label, any of the labels assigned is counted as a correct prediction for evaluation.
- `disagree_bin`: predict 1 if there is disagreement between annotators on 0 versus all other labels and predict 0 otherwise.

System performance on all five predicted labels was evaluated using F1 macro score over all classes. The final score which was used for ranking the submissions was calculated as the unweighted average over all 5 scores.

Subtask 2: Label distribution prediction In subtask 2 the goal was to predict the distribution for each text in a dataset where the target distribution is derived from the original distribution of labels assigned by several human annotators. The annotators assigned (according to the annotation guidelines) the strength of misogyny/sexism present in the given text via the labels 0 (for no sexism present) to 4 (extreme sexism). From the set of assigned labels, two target distributions where derived: a binarized version, specifying the fractions of annotators who assigned 0 and who assigned non-0 labels, and another distribution with the fractions of annotators who assigned labels 0 to 4. The participants had to submit a dataset which contained, for each example in the test set, the predicted fractions for both distributions.

For the evaluation of subtask 2, the Jensen-Shannon (JS) divergence between the target distribution and the predicted distribution was calculated and averaged for each of the binary and the multiclass distributions in the test set and the two JS divergences where then averaged to obtain the final score. The JS-divergence was chosen as it is a true metric and bounded, and it is therefore well suited to be used and combined into the final score.

Closed versus open tracks For each subtask, there was a closed and an open track. In the closed track, neither additional data labelled for sexism or misogyny, nor language models or embeddings which might have been pre-trained or instruction-finetuned with sexism/misogyny specific data were allowed to enhance reproducability.[4] For the open track, participants were encouraged to use whatever approach they preferred. However, only the closed track counted towards the competition of the shared task and a closed track submission was required for the submission of a paper.

3.2 Task Organisation

The GermEval2024 Shared Task GerMS-Detect was run on Codabench and organised in four different competitions: subtask 1 – closed track[5], subtask 1 – open track[6], subtask 2 – closed track[7], and subtask 2 – open track[8]. Reason for this was to keep the leader boards and the evaluation metrics separate. The task was organised in three phases: a trial phase, a development phase, and a competition phase (which ended on 2024-06-28). In the trial phase, an initial set of 1000 labeled training examples and 500 unlabeled test examples was available, in the development phase 4486 labeled training examples and 1512 unlabeled test examples were available and in the competition phase, 5998 labeled training examples and 1986 unlabeled test ex-

[4]For more details, see `https://ofai.github.io/GermEval2024-GerMS/closed-track.html`

[5]`https://www.codabench.org/competitions/2744/`

[6]`https://www.codabench.org/competitions/2745/`

[7]`https://www.codabench.org/competitions/2746/`

[8]`https://www.codabench.org/competitions/2747/`

amples were available. Each training set contained the labeled test data from the previous phase. All data is available from the GermEval2004 GerMS-Detect web site[9]. The training/test data splits were carried out in a way that simultanously stratified the distribution of annotator ids, class labels, and original annotation rounds (i.e., source of the data) as much as possible. The code used for evaluation is available from the GermEval GerMS-Detect Github repository[10].

4 Participant Systems and Results

Per subtask and track, one submission account was allowed per team. 13 teams registered for the shared task, of these, during the competition phase, 7 submitted to subtask 1 – closed track, 3 submitted to subtask 1 – open track, 6 submitted to subtask 2 – closed track and 2 submitted to subtask 2 – open track. 5 teams submitted papers describing their approaches and results, which will be discussed in the following chapters.

4.1 Leader Board Results

In the closed track, the 5 teams which submitted a paper were also the ones which achieved the highest results on the leader board, see Table 2 for a summary of their results.

Team	ST1-c F1 macro	ST1-o F1 macro	ST2-c JS	ST2-o JS
THAugs	0.642	-	-	-
ficode	0.641	-	0.354	-
Quabynar77	0.611	0.452	0.292	0.409
Team GDA	0.597	0.586	0.301	-
pd2904	0.483	-	0.388	-

Table 2: Top ranked leaderboard results and summary statistics for subtask 1 (ST1) and subtask 2 (ST2), the open track (o) and the closed track (c) of the 5 teams who submitted a paper. The best submission is marked in red.

Subtask 1 All five teams developed systems for subtask 1 - closed. The scores obtained by their best submissions are shown in Figure 4 with their p=0.05 confidence intervals[11]. At p=0.05 the best two submissions were not significantly different. For both submissions an ensemble method fine-tuning Deepset's `gbert-large`[12] (teams THAugs and ficode) was employed. The third best submission by team Quabynar fine-tuned Deepset's `gbert-base`[13]. The fourth best submission by team GDA employed a Support Vector Machine (SVM) classifier on top of `mE5-large` embeddings[14]. The fifth best submission by team pd2904 followed a more traditional approach by applying a combination of Random Forests, Light Gradient-Boosting, Extreme Gradient Boosting, SVM, and CatBoost models.

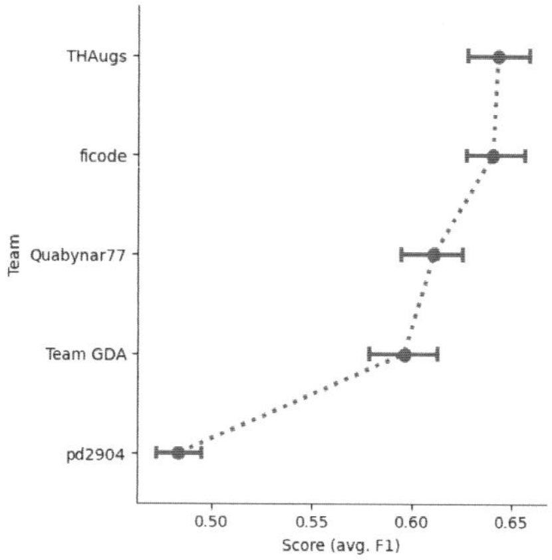

Figure 4: Comparison of results showing $p = 0.05$ confidence intervals of the teams who participated in subtask 1 closed.

Two teams additionally submitted results for the open track of subtask 1 (team GDA and Quabynar77). However, only team Quabynar described their approach for the open track in their paper. They applied few-shot learning on OpenAI's GPT 3.5 Turbo by selecting only the top 5 comments iteratively for each annotator, achieving an F1 macro score of 0.452.

Subtask 2 Four teams submitted results for subtask 2, see Figure 5 for an overview of their results. The top submission by team Quabynar77 fine-tuned Google's `bert-base-german-cased`[15]. The second best approach by team GDA employed a Support Vector Machine classifier with `gbert-large-pc` embeddings[16]. An

[9] `https://ofai.github.io/GermEval2024-GerMS/`
[10] `https://github.com/OFAI/GermEval2024-GerMS/tree/main/python`
[11] Calculated via bootstrapping of 500 samples using the CompStats (Nava-Muñoz et al., 2024) package, see `https://compstats.readthedocs.io/en/latest/`
[12] `https://huggingface.co/deepset/gbert-large`
[13] `https://huggingface.co/deepset/gbert-base`
[14] `https://huggingface.co/intfloat/multilingual-e5-large`
[15] `https://huggingface.co/google-bert/bert-base-german-cased`
[16] `https://huggingface.co/deutsche-telekom/gbert-large-paraphrase-cosine`

interesting difference between the two top submissions is that the approach fine-tuning `bert-base-german-cased` achieved the same result for the multi score distribution as the SVN classifier with `gbert-large-pc` embeddings, but performed better on the binary distribution: JS divergence = 0.248 (team Quabynar77) vs. 0.267 (team GDA).

Team ficode used the same ensemble method as in subtask 1, fine-tuning `gbert-large`. Team pd2904 also employed a similar approach as in subtask 1 by training the same types of traditional models for each annotator.

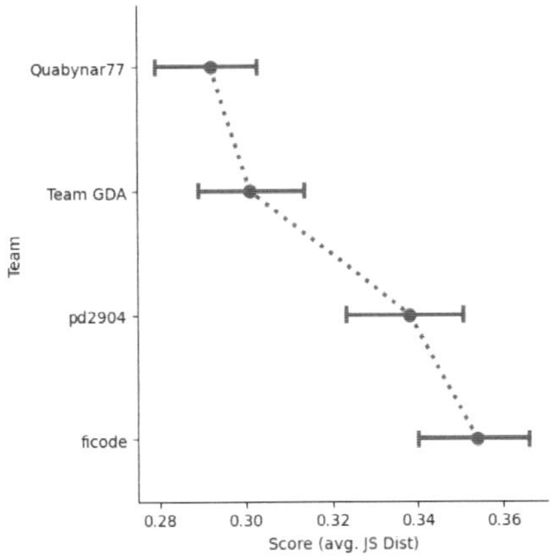

Figure 5: Comparison of results showing $p = 0.05$ confidence intervals of the teams who participated in subtask 2 closed.

Team Quabynar was the only team participating in the open track of subtask 2 who described their results in their paper. They applied the same approach as for the open track of subtask 1, using few-shot learning on OpenAI's GPT 3.5 Turbo (iteratively selecting the top 5 comments for each annotator), performing worse than all submissions of the closed track of subtask 2, i.e., achieving a higher score for the JS divergence.

5 Conclusion

In this paper, we presented an extended dataset based on Krenn et al. (2024) with a higher number of expert annotations, which allows training a classifier directly on the individual labels.

Further, we analysed and discussed annotator variation in detail and proposed a qualitative method to gain further insights in reasons for annotator variation, which might also be relevant for other datasets with significant annotator disagreement.

Additionally, we summarized the systems of teams submitting a paper to describe their approach. Four out of five teams used transformer architectures. German versions of BERT were the most popular models, but also multilingual-e5-large embeddings were employed. However, also submitted were results from a transformer based approach combined with a SVM classifier on top, as well as an approach based on traditional models (Random Forests, Light Gradient-Boosting, Extreme Gradient Boosting, SVM, and CatBoost models).

6 Limitations

Even though there are more *not sexist* comments in the dataset than *sexist* comments, the dataset has a selection bias towards sexist comments (see the description of the data collection in section 2), which makes the proportion of sexist comments much higher than in the news fora. Therefore a classifier trained on that data might label a comment as *sexist* with a higher probability. However, if the proportion of *sexist* comments would have reflected the proportion in the real data, a much larger amount of data would have needed labelling in order to span such a broad range of topics.

The comments in the dataset are annotated without further context, e.g., the article a forum is related to, or the thread a comment is part of. Therefore some *sexist* comments might be missed due to the lack of context. Also, ironic comments responding to a *sexist* comment might be misinterpreted as *sexist*.

The specific newspaper's forum moderation policy influenced the annotation guidelines and also the majority of the annotators were employed as forum moderators for that specific newspaper. In other contexts, other criteria for identifying sexism or misogyny might be relevant.

A limitation of the shared task is that submissions to open tracks did not count towards the competition ranking and closed track submissions were required for a paper submission. We only received one description of an approach for the open track, which is not sufficient for a proper comparison between the closed and the open track. However, the reason for emphasizing on the closed task was reproducibility.

7 Ethical Considerations

The foremost goal of the dataset collection was to train classifiers that support content moderators of an Austrian German language online newspaper with regards to identifying sexist and misogynous comments. In the forum of this online newspaper, 20K to 50K comments are made per day (with rising tendency), making solely manual monitoring for human moderators impossible. Therefore, support by automatic monitoring of classifiers is a precondition for moderators to intervene in a timely manner.

There is risk of harm to annotators by repeated exposure to sexist and misogynist utterances. Even though annotators are either professional forum moderators used to handling sexist and misogynous comments, or experts in corpus annotation, regular monitoring is necessary to watch for negative effects of excessive exposure to harmful content on individuals. Researchers and developers might be affected by the exposure to harmful content, as well as readers of the paper. The exposure to such harmful content may also lead to prejudiced discussions and the reproduction or reinforcement of harmful representation stereotypes. Therefore, content warnings are placed at the beginning of the paper before examples for *sexist* comments are presented, cf. (Kirk et al., 2022).

Violation of privacy is a risk which may concern forum users who are mentioned in the comments or whose comments are part of the dataset. As a countermeasure, all potential user names, at-mentions, URLs, email addresses were deleted.

A datasheet was published together with the dataset on huggingface to offer detailed information on the capacities and limitations of the dataset. The advantage of making the dataset publicly available is that fellow researchers can take up and further extend the work. We strongly recommend to publish a model card (Mitchell et al., 2019) with each model trained on the dataset. Still, misuse of the dataset can not be completely ruled out.

Acknowledgments

This work was conducted as part of the projects FemDwell[17] supported through FemPower IKT 2018[18] and EKIP – A Platform for Ethical AI Application[19] supported by the Austrian Research Promotion Agency (FFG)[20]. We thank the forum moderators at derStandard.at for their contributions to developing the annotation guidelines and their efforts in annotating the dataset.

References

Gavin Abercrombie, Valerio Basile, Sara Tonelli, Verena Rieser, and Alexandra Uma. 2022. Proceedings of the 1st workshop on perspectivist approaches to nlp@ lrec2022. In *Proceedings of the 1st Workshop on Perspectivist Approaches to NLP@ LREC2022*.

Valerio Basile, Cristina Bosco, Elisabetta Fersini, Debora Nozza, Viviana Patti, Francisco Manuel Rangel Pardo, Paolo Rosso, and Manuela Sanguinetti. 2019. Semeval-2019 task 5: Multilingual detection of hate speech against immigrants and women in twitter. In *Proceedings of the 13th international workshop on semantic evaluation*, pages 54–63.

Aida Mostafazadeh Davani, Mark Díaz, and Vinodkumar Prabhakaran. 2022. Dealing with disagreements: Looking beyond the majority vote in subjective annotations. *Transactions of the Association for Computational Linguistics*, 10:92–110.

Elisabetta Fersini, Paolo Rosso, Maria Anzovino, et al. 2018. Overview of the task on automatic misogyny identification at ibereval 2018. *Ibereval@ sepln*, 2150:214–228.

Andrew F Hayes and Klaus Krippendorff. 2007. Answering the call for a standard reliability measure for coding data. *Communication methods and measures*, 1(1):77–89.

Hannah Kirk, Abeba Birhane, Bertie Vidgen, and Leon Derczynski. 2022. Handling and presenting harmful text in nlp research. In *Findings of the Association for Computational Linguistics: EMNLP 2022*, pages 497–510.

Hannah Kirk, Wenjie Yin, Bertie Vidgen, and Paul Röttger. 2023. SemEval-2023 task 10: Explainable detection of online sexism. In *Proceedings of SemEval-2023*, pages 2193–2210, Toronto, Canada.

Brigitte Krenn, Johann Petrak, Marina Kubina, and Christian Burger. 2024. Germs-at: A sexism/misogyny dataset of forum comments from an austrian online newspaper. In *Proceedings of the 2024 Joint International Conference on Computational Linguistics, Language Resources and Evaluation (LREC-COLING 2024)*, pages 7728–7739.

Philipp Mayring. 2014. *Qualitative content analysis: theoretical foundation, basic procedures and software solution*. Klagenfurt, AUT.

[17] `https://ofai.github.io/femdwell/`

[18] `https://austrianstartups.com/event/call-fempower-ikt-2018`

[19] `https://ekip.ai/`

[20] `https://www.ffg.at/en`

Margaret Mitchell, Simone Wu, Andrew Zaldivar, Parker Barnes, Lucy Vasserman, Ben Hutchinson, Elena Spitzer, Inioluwa Deborah Raji, and Timnit Gebru. 2019. Model cards for model reporting. In *Proceedings of the conference on fairness, accountability, and transparency*, pages 220–229.

Sergio Nava-Muñoz, Mario Graff, and Hugo Jair Escalante. 2024. Analysis of systems' performance in natural language processing competitions. *Pattern Recognition Letters*.

Atul Kr Ojha, A Seza Doğruöz, Giovanni Da San Martino, Harish Tayyar Madabushi, Ritesh Kumar, and Elisa Sartori. 2023. Proceedings of the 17th international workshop on semantic evaluation (semeval-2023). In *Proceedings of the 17th International Workshop on Semantic Evaluation (SemEval-2023)*.

Ellie Pavlick and Tom Kwiatkowski. 2019. Inherent disagreements in human textual inferences. *Transactions of the Association for Computational Linguistics*, 7:677–694.

Barbara Plank. 2022. The "problem" of human label variation: On ground truth in data, modeling and evaluation. In *Proceedings of the 2022 Conference on Empirical Methods in Natural Language Processing*, pages 10671–10682.

Paul Röttger, Bertie Vidgen, Dirk Hovy, and Janet Pierrehumbert. 2022. Two contrasting data annotation paradigms for subjective nlp tasks. In *Proceedings of the 2022 Conference of the North American Chapter of the Association for Computational Linguistics: Human Language Technologies*, pages 175–190.

Marta Sandri, Elisa Leonardelli, Sara Tonelli, and Elisabetta Ježek. 2023. Why don't you do it right? analysing annotators' disagreement in subjective tasks. In *Proceedings of the 17th Conference of the European Chapter of the Association for Computational Linguistics*, pages 2428–2441.

Alexandra Uma, Tommaso Fornaciari, Anca Dumitrache, Tristan Miller, Jon Chamberlain, Barbara Plank, Edwin Simpson, and Massimo Poesio. 2021a. Semeval-2021 task 12: Learning with disagreements. In *Proceedings of the 15th International Workshop on Semantic Evaluation (SemEval-2021)*, pages 338–347.

Alexandra N Uma, Tommaso Fornaciari, Dirk Hovy, Silviu Paun, Barbara Plank, and Massimo Poesio. 2021b. Learning from disagreement: A survey. *Journal of Artificial Intelligence Research*, 72:1385–1470.

THAugs at GermEval 2024 (Shared Task 1: GerMS-Detect): Predicting the Severity of Misogyny/Sexism in Forum Comments with BERT Models (Subtask 1, Closed Track and Additional Experiments)

Corsin Geiss and **Alessandra Zarcone**
Technische Hochschule Augsburg
An der Hochschule 1, 86161 Augsburg, Germany
corsin.geiss@tha.de, alessandra.zarcone@tha.de

Abstract

We present our approach and results for Shared Task 1 of the GermEval2024 competition (GerMS-Detect), in particular Subtask 1, aimed at predicting the severity of misogyny/sexism in text from Austrian online fora. We start from a German BERT-based baseline and a multilingual BERT-based baseline and compare them with a series of finetuned BERT-based models, in order to assess the contribution of (1) finetuning on further data from a high-quality misogyny detection dataset for a different language (Danish) and (2) finetuning on a more generic hate speech dataset for German. The best results, however, were obtained by adapting the `deepset/gbert-large` model to task-specific data, without finetuning on external data, using a weighted loss function and k-fold cross-validation, which resulted in an F1 score of 0.643 and was our submission for the Closed Track. Our findings highlight the complexity of detecting nuanced forms of hate speech and the importance of models adapted to the specific contexts of use.

1 Introduction

In recent years, social media platforms and online news websites have become central mediums for discussing a wide array of topics with a global audience. Various entities, including companies, shops, and TV shows, use these platforms to present content and interact with followers. However, the anonymity afforded by the internet often leads to various forms of harmful content, including sexist and misogynistic expressions, ranging from subtle biases to toxic comments directed at individuals or groups (Van Royen et al., 2017). This can lead to a normalization of misogynistic anti-minority speech, which can in turn perpetuate discrimination (Beukeboom and Burgers, 2019) and even increase the incidence of hate crime and sexual violence (Müller and Schwarz, 2023).

A possible way to address these issues is through automated detection of sexist and misogynistic content, which can support moderation efforts across the spectrum of harmful expressions. A series of GermEval shared tasks evaluation has focused on offensive language detection for the German language in Twitter data (Wiegand et al., 2018; Struß et al., 2019) and Facebook user comments (Risch et al., 2021). The Shared Task 1 at GermEval 2024 poses the challenge of detecting sexism in Austrian news comment as well as the majority grading (Subtask 1) and grading distribution (Subtask 2).

Detecting misogyny and sexism in text from online platforms in German is inherently challenging. Hate speech detection in online platforms for a specific language requires adapting existing models to the specific language, domain, and task, considering the full range of sexist and misogynistic expressions (Karan and Šnajder, 2018). Additionally, as sexist content can range from subtle implications to extremely toxic and violent expressions, annotators typically diverge in their opinions and perceptions of what constitutes misogynistic or sexist language (Stappen et al., 2021).

Furthermore, biases in datasets, such as those created by focused sampling instead of random sampling, can further complicate detection and result in lower classification scores under realistic settings (Wiegand et al., 2019). Unintended biases in misogyny detection models, such as those caused by identity terms, can lead to the misclassification of non-misogynistic content as misogynistic, highlighting the complexity of creating fair and effective detection systems (Nozza et al., 2019).

We present our approach and results for the 2024 GerMS-Detect Competition (GermEval2024, Shared Task 1, Subtask 1). Our starting point are pre-trained encoder-only transformed models (BERT, Devlin et al., 2019) which have shown to be successful in various NLP challenges (Min et al., 2023). The first question we address is whether a multilingual BERT model can leverage existing task-specific data in a different language (Danish) to bring an advantage over a language-specific German BERT model. The second question is whether language-specific data for finetuning can be extracted from a more generic German hate speech dataset.

Our best-performing model, a finetuned German BERT model, achieved an F1 Score of 0.643 and was submitted to the Closed Track, as it did not use any additional training data. This model was trained using a weighted loss function to handle class imbalance and evaluated through a k-fold cross-validation approach (with $k = 5$). To further enhance the robustness of our predictions, we employed an ensemble method, combining the five best models from cross-validation.

The multilingual BERT model with additional training showed some improvements compared to its corresponding baseline, but still performed worse than the basic version of the German BERT model `deepset/gbert-large` with simple language-modeling finetuning.

We additionally evaluated the contribution of a German hate speech dataset, which was filtered using cosine similarity of sentence embeddings (Reimers and Gurevych, 2019), aiming to select the most relevant training data for misogyny/sexism detection. This experiment did not yield improvements in model performance either.

These experiments provided insights that simply filtering for misogyny is insufficient for capturing the specific nuances of sexism and the differing opinions of annotators. This highlighted the complexity of the task, where understanding the context and subjective interpretations of sexism is crucial.

Our code is released on Github for further research and development.[1]

2 Related Work

The detection of hate speech on social media platforms, as well as the detection of more subtle forms of toxicity and prejudice, including sexist and misogynistic content (ranging from subtle biases to overt violence), has been a significant research area due to its societal impact. Various studies have utilized different methodologies and datasets to address these issues. Poletto et al. (2021) provide a systematic review of resources and benchmark corpora for hate speech detection, which highlights the variety of datasets available for training and evaluating hate speech detection models.

When it comes to misogyny detection, previous work has typically focused on Twitter (Anzovino et al., 2018; Jha and Mamidi, 2017) or Reddit (Farrell et al., 2019; Guest et al., 2021). The need for annotated datasets in multiple languages is underscored by Arango Monnar et al. (2022), who highlights the limitations of existing resources and emphasize the importance of cross-lingual and cross-cultural perspectives in developing hate speech detection models.

Transformer-based models, particularly BERT, have revolutionized NLP with their ability to capture contextual information bidirectionally, significantly improving performance across various NLP tasks (Devlin et al., 2019). The success of these models has prompted their application for hate speech detection, including misogyny and sexism (Pamungkas et al., 2020; Kalra and Zubiaga, 2021; Safi Samghabadi et al., 2020). When it comes to pretrained encoders, multilingual models may be suitable for leveraging cross-lingual information and for exploiting existing datasets in a language different than the target language (Muller et al., 2021). It seems however that language-specific models outperform multilingual ones for tasks involving nuanced language understanding (Zeinert et al., 2021; Rust et al., 2021).

Handling class imbalance is a critical aspect of developing robust models for hate speech detection. Younes and Mathiak (2022) explored the use of pre-trained language models and weighted loss functions to address class imbalance, showing significant improvements in model performance for underrepresented classes. These techniques are essential for ensuring that models do not overlook minority classes, which is a common issue in hate speech detection (Kwarteng et al., 2022).

Ensemble learning techniques have been explored to enhance the performance of hate speech detection models. Mazari et al. (2024) demonstrated the effectiveness of combining BERT with other models through ensemble methods, achieving significant improvements in detecting multiple aspects of hate speech. This approach leverages the strengths of different models to provide more robust and accurate predictions.

[1] `https://github.com/tha-atlas/GermEval2024-THAugs/`

3 Data, Tasks and Evaluation

3.1 GERMS-AT dataset

The data for the GermEval2024 Shared Task 1 (GerMS-Detect) came from the GERMS-AT dataset (Krenn et al., 2024). It consists of comments from an Austrian online newspaper. The comments were annotated by multiple annotators with regards to the severity of misogyny/sexism present in text, on a scale from 0 to 4, where 0 represents no sexism/misogyny, and 4 indicates extreme sexism/misogyny. The labels capture the distribution and variability of annotators' opinions.

The datasets were released in three phases: Trial, Development, and Competition[2]. Each phase provided training and testing data, with the test data from one phase becoming part of the labeled training data in the next phase, along with the previous phase's training data. In the Competition Phase, the training data included 5,598 comments (including the labeled test data from the Development Phase and the training data from both the Trial and Development phases), with 4,221 labeled as non-sexist and 1,377 as sexist (majority label). The testing data for the Competition Phase comprised 1,986 unlabeled comments.

Content warning: We report examples of sexist and misogynous language to illustrate the data.

Below are two examples that reflect the range of severity captured in the dataset:

- **Original:** "Ja - weils politisch-medial nicht gewünscht ist gemischte Ranglisten zu zeigen bei denen Frauen auf den vorderen Plätzen nicht auftauchen."
  Translation: "Yes - because it is not politically or media-wise desired to show mixed rankings where women do not appear in the top positions."
  Majority Label: 1 (Low Severity)

- **Original:** "wegen der paar frauen die es aus der küche heraus schaffen eine eigene karriere zu starten ist es eigentlich ein overkill eine eigene genderform zu schaffen. der überwiegende teil der frauen freut sich wenn man(n) ! sie regelmäßig ob der hervorzüglich gekochten speisen lobt."
  Translation: "Because of the few women who manage to start their own careers outside of the kitchen, it is actually overkill to create a separate gender form. The majority of women are happy when (a man) regularly praises them for the excellently cooked meals."
  Majority Label: 4 (Extreme Severity)

[2] https://ofai.github.io/GermEval2024-GerMS/, Accessed: 2024-07-02

The dataset is presented in JSONL format, each entry contains:

- **id**: A unique identifier for the comment.
- **text**: The text of the comment.
- **annotations**: An array of dictionaries (only in the labeled dataset), each containing:
  - **user**: An anonymized ID for the annotator (e.g., "A003").
  - **label**: The label assigned by the annotator.
- **annotators**: An array of annotator IDs who labeled the example (only in the unlabeled dataset).

Figure 1 shows the distribution of the misogyny/sexism severity labels in the dataset, considering all labels provided by the annotators. As illustrated, there is a significant class imbalance, with the majority of comments labeled as "None" (label 0), and fewer comments labeled with higher severity levels.

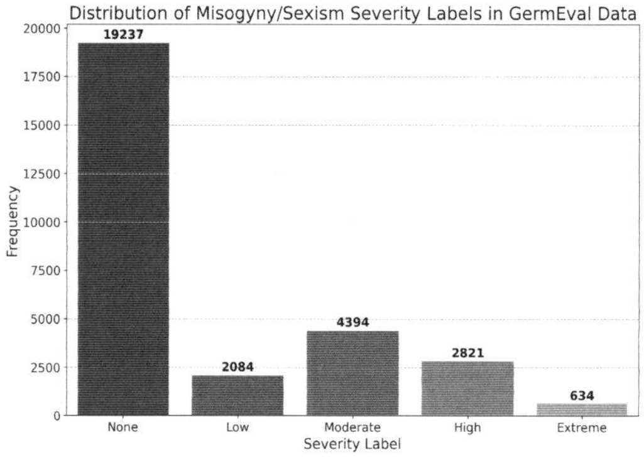

Figure 1: Distribution of misogyny/sexism severity labels in the GermEval2024/GerMS-Detect Data, considering all annotator labels.

3.2 Additional Datasets

To explore potential improvements brought by finetuning on more data, we incorporated two additional datasets containing annotated examples of hate speech:

- **Bajer Dataset**: This dataset contains annotated Danish social media posts labeled for misogyny. It includes high-quality annotations of online misogynistic content, providing insights into cross-lingual and cross-cultural aspects of misogyny detection (Zeinert et al., 2021).

- **GAHD Dataset**: The German Adversarial Hate Speech Dataset (GAHD) contains adversarial examples aimed at improving model robustness in detecting hate speech (Goldzycher et al., 2024). This dataset includes texts labeled as hate speech or not.

These datasets were not used in our submission to the Closed Track.

3.3 Data Preprocessing

The preprocessing steps were consistently applied across all stages of our methodology to ensure clean input text. These steps included removing HTML tags, URLs, emojis, and extra whitespaces (Glazkova, 2023). This preprocessing was performed on all datasets used, including the GermEval2024/GerMS-Detect Data, the Danish sexism dataset, and the German adversarial hate speech dataset (GAHD).

3.4 Task Description

In Subtask 1, the goal is to predict the severity of misogyny/sexism for each text based on the labels assigned by multiple annotators. The labels reflect different strategies for combining multiple annotations into a single target label:

- **bin_maj**: Predict 1 if a majority of annotators assigned a label other than 0, otherwise predict 0. Both 1 and 0 are correct if there's no majority.

- **bin_one**: Predict 1 if at least one annotator assigned a label other than 0, otherwise predict 0.

- **bin_all**: Predict 1 if all annotators assigned labels other than 0, otherwise predict 0.

- **multi_maj**: Predict the majority label if there is one; if no majority, any of the labels assigned is counted as correct.

- **disagree_bin**: Predict 1 if there is disagreement on 0 versus all other labels, otherwise predict 0.

3.5 Evaluation

System performance on all five predicted labels (bin_maj, bin_one, bin_all, multi_maj, disagree_bin) is evaluated using the F1 macro score over all classes. The final score (which is used for ranking submissions in the leaderboard) is calculated as the unweighted average over all five scores.

4 Methodology

4.1 Model Architecture

The model architecture used for the final finetuning on the training data is consistent across all our BERT-based models and is designed to handle the specific requirements of the classification tasks. The architecture includes the following components:

- **Input Layer**: Handles tokenized input text, including input IDs and attention masks.

- **BERT Layer**: Utilizes a pretrained BERT model to extract contextual embeddings from the input text. We used the following BERT models in this layer (more details on the models in 4.6-4.7):
  - **deepset/gbert-large**: A German BERT model finetuned for specific language tasks.
  - **google-bert/bert-base-cased**: A base BERT model suitable for general language understanding tasks in German.
  - **bert-base-multilingual-cased**: A multilingual BERT model capable of handling multiple languages, including German.

- **Fully Connected Layers**: Consists of multiple fully connected layers with batch normalization and activation functions.

- **Classifiers**: Comprises several task-specific classifiers for binary and multi-class classification.

The architecture is illustrated in Figure 2.

4.2 Cross-Validation

To ensure model robustness, we employed k-fold cross-validation (with $k = 5$), partitioning the dataset into five subsets, training on four, and validating on one. This process was repeated five times with different validation subsets, and performance metrics were averaged. Stratified splitting ensured

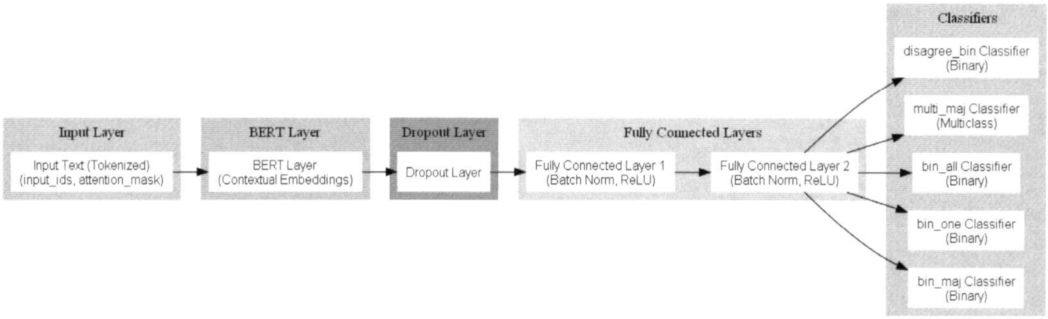

Figure 2: Model architecture used for the finetuning process.

balanced class representation across folds. Except for the final submission, we used the GermEval development data and test data for training and testing. The primary evaluation metric was the F1 score, chosen for its balance between precision and recall, suitable for imbalanced datasets (Sokolova and Lapalme, 2009).

4.3 Ensemble Learning

To enhance prediction robustness, we employed an ensemble learning approach. Our ensemble consisted of five models, each trained on a different fold of the dataset using 5-fold cross-validation. This approach ensures that each model is exposed to a slightly different subset of the training data, potentially capturing different aspects of the problem.

The models in the ensemble shared the same architecture (described in Section 4.1) but differed in their learned parameters due to being trained on different data folds. For prediction, we used the following process:

1. Each of the five models made predictions on the test data independently.

2. For binary classification tasks (bin_maj, bin_one, bin_all, disagree_bin), the raw logits were transformed using a sigmoid function to obtain probability scores.

3. For the multi-class task (multi_maj), a softmax function was applied to the logits to obtain class probabilities.

4. The predictions from all five models were aggregated by averaging the probability scores for each task.

5. For binary tasks, the final prediction was determined by rounding the average probability (threshold of 0.5).

6. For the multi-class task, the class with the highest average probability was selected as the final prediction.

This ensemble approach mitigates individual model variability and improves overall performance by leveraging the collective wisdom of multiple models. The use of probability averaging allows for a more nuanced final prediction, potentially capturing uncertainties that a single model might miss (Mazari et al., 2024).

4.4 Handling Class Imbalance

In order to address class imbalance, we employed a weighted loss function (Younes and Mathiak, 2022), assigning higher weights to underrepresented classes to prevent model bias towards frequent classes.

4.5 Hyperparameter Tuning

For hyperparameter tuning and architecture building, we initially used the `google-bert/bert-base-cased` model[3], due to its lower resource requirements compared to `deepset/gbert-large` (Chan et al., 2020)[4]. We employed Optuna (Akiba et al., 2019), a hyperparameter optimization framework, to efficiently search for optimal hyperparameters. Our search focused on learning rate, batch size, weight decay, hidden layer dimensions, dropout rate, and number of epochs. The search ranges were informed by previous experience with similar

[3] `https://huggingface.co/google-bert/bert-base-german-cased`, Accessed: 2024-06-25

[4] `https://huggingface.co/deepset/gbert-large`, Accessed: 2024-06-25

tasks and models. Approximately 50 trials were conducted using Optuna's Bayesian optimization approach, as shown in Table 1.

The model was trained using the AdamW optimizer (Loshchilov and Hutter, 2019), with a ReduceLROnPlateau scheduler (PyTorch Documentation, 2021) to adjust the learning rate during training. For the final `deepset/gbert-large` model used in the competition, we had to adjust some parameters due to GPU memory constraints and the larger model size. Specifically, we reduced the batch size to 16 and adjusted the learning rate to 1×10^{-5}. We used the development training data for hyperparameter tuning

4.6 Closed Track Approaches

4.6.1 Baseline Models

German Baseline We utilized the `german bert cased` model as a baseline to compare the performance of our finetuned models. This model was chosen due to its lower resource requirements and effectiveness in handling German language tasks.

Multilingual Baseline The `bert multilingual` model was used as a baseline for assessing cross-lingual transfer learning capabilities (Devlin et al., 2019). It provided a benchmark for evaluating improvements from finetuning on a dataset in a different language than the target language.

4.6.2 Finetuning German Models

Finetuning `gbert-large` We performed language model finetuning (LM finetuning) on the `deepset/gbert-large` model (Chan et al., 2020) using the GermEval2024 dataset. This step adapted the model to the specific language and context of the GermEval data, enhancing its understanding of the linguistic characteristics of the domain.

Finetuning `german bert cased` We also performed LM-finetuning on the `german bert cased` model using the same dataset. This model served as a point of comparison to evaluate the performance gains achieved from the LM-finetuning process itself.

4.6.3 Finetuning Process Details

For both models, we used a custom dataset class and `BertTokenizer` to tokenize the preprocessed texts, ensuring consistent input size by truncating and padding them to a maximum length. We initialized the `BertForMaskedLM` model, setting up the training environment with specific arguments such as epochs, batch size, and learning rate. A data collator dynamically created masked language modeling data during training. Using the `Trainer` class from the Transformers library, we managed the training loop, including forward and backward passes, optimization, and checkpointing. Post-training, we saved the finetuned models and tokenizers for the classification task.

4.7 Additional Experiments

4.7.1 Harvesting Data for Task-Based Finetuning

To prepare the filtered GAHD dataset for finetuning, we performed a detailed data harvesting process, aimed at finding datapoints which were not just examples of hate speech, but specifically examples of sexism/misogyny:

1. **Data Preparation**: We read the GermEval data, labeled each entry as sexist or non-sexist based on the annotations, and split the dataset into training and test sets to find an optimal threshold for identifying misogynistic content, aiming for a precision value of about 75%.

2. **Model Setup and Finetuning**: We used sentence embeddings (Reimers and Gurevych, 2019) from the T-Systems-onsite/cross-en-de-roberta-sentence-transformer model[5] and finetuned it on the GermEval data to improve the filtering process. The known sexist sentences were all the sexist sentences from GermEval.

3. **Similarity Calculation**: We computed the cosine similarity between the embeddings of the GAHD dataset texts and the known sexist sentences from GermEval.

4. **Filtering**: Using the determined threshold of 0.14, we filtered the GAHD dataset to retain texts with high cosine similarity scores, indicating misogynistic content.

It's important to note that the filtering process may sometimes incorrectly classify certain sentences. For example:

Content warning: We report examples of sexist and misogynous language to analyse model errors.

- **Original:** "Sollten wir nicht zumindest versuchen, diesen Thread in etwas Positives

[5] https://huggingface.co/T-Systems-onsite/cross-en-de-roberta-sentence-transformer, Accessed: 2024-06-25

Hyperparameter	Search Range	Optimal Value
Batch size	[16, 32, 64]	64
Learning rate	$[1 \times 10^{-5}, 5 \times 10^{-5}]$	4.053×10^{-5}
Weight decay	$[0.1, 0.3]$	0.2019
Hidden layer dimension 1	[512, 768, 1024]	768
Hidden layer dimension 2	[128, 256, 512]	256
Dropout rate	[0.1, 0.5]	0.3606
Number of epochs	[8, 12]	12

Table 1: Hyperparameter search ranges and optimal values

umzuwandeln, etwa Möglichkeiten, weiße Männer und Frauen vor gemischten Beziehungen zu retten?"
Translation: "Shouldn't we at least try to turn this thread into something positive, such as ways to save white men and women from mixed relationships?"
(This sentence may be incorrectly classified due to the word "Frauen" (women) despite the context not being inherently misogynistic.)

- **Original:** "Ich habe 2019 auf TIK TOK einige SEHR SCHÖNE UND HEISSE SEXY MÄDCHEN VON MUSICALLY gefunden, schade, dass sie alle wie Huren wirken"
Translation: "In 2019, I found some VERY BEAUTIFUL AND HOT SEXY GIRLS from Musical.ly on TikTok, it's a shame that they all seem like whores"
(This sentence is correctly identified as sexist due to explicit objectification and derogatory language towards women.)

The final filtered GAHD subset, balanced to include an equal number of sexist and non-sexist examples, contained 769 sentences of each type and was saved for further finetuning.

4.7.2 Finetuning on Filtered GAHD Dataset

To improve its ability to detect misogynistic content, we finetuned the `german bert cased` model on the filtered GAHD dataset prepared in the previous step. The finetuning process involved tokenizing the text, computing class weights to address class imbalance, and training the model using the AdamW optimizer with a set of hyperparameters tailored for this specific task.

4.8 Finetuning Multilingual Models

To assess the multilingual BERT model's cross-lingual transfer learning capability, we performed task-based finetuning on a Danish sexism dataset (Zeinert et al., 2021). The multilingual BERT model was finetuned on the Danish dataset with the following setup:

- Learning rate: 2×10^{-5}
- Batch size: 16
- Number of epochs: 1
- Dropout rates: 0.3 for hidden and attention layers
- Optimizer: AdamW
- Evaluation metrics: Accuracy, F1 score, precision, and recall.

This evaluation aimed to determine if finetuning on Danish data could lead to performance improvements on German language tasks.

5 Results

Table 2 summarizes the F1 scores achieved by different models and configurations during our exploration and experimentation. These models were trained on the GermEval Development data and tested on the GermEval Development test data.

5.1 Closed Track Results

5.1.1 german bert cased (baseline)

The `german bert cased` model, without any finetuning, served as our primary baseline. It achieved an average F1 score of 0.5825 across all tasks, providing a solid starting point for comparison.

5.1.2 bert multilingual (baseline)

Our multilingual baseline, using the `bert-base-multilingual-cased` model without finetuning, achieved an average F1 score of 0.5679. This performance was slightly lower than the German-specific baseline, highlighting the potential benefits of language-specific models for this task.

Model	bin_maj	bin_one	bin_all	multi_maj	disagree_bin	**Avg. F1 Score**
`gbert-large (LM-finetuned)`	0.7347	0.7707	0.7132	0.2886	0.6132	0.6241
`german bert cased (LM-finetuned)`	0.7069	0.7532	0.6459	0.2778	0.6085	0.5985
`german bert cased (baseline)`	0.6865	0.7299	0.6632	0.2669	0.5660	0.5825
`german bert cased (task-finetuned on GAHD)`	0.6834	0.7180	0.6477	0.2693	0.5700	0.5777
`bert multilingual (baseline)`	0.6769	0.7301	0.6000	0.2467	0.5858	0.5679
`bert multilingual (task-finetuned on Danish)`	0.6776	0.7328	0.6185	0.2518	0.6061	0.5773

Table 2: F1 scores achieved by different models and configurations during exploration and experimentation. These models were trained on the GermEval Development data and tested on the GermEval Development test data.

5.1.3 german bert cased (LM-finetuned)

After language model finetuning, the `german bert cased` model showed improved performance, with an average F1 score of 0.5985. This improvement demonstrates the effectiveness of adapting the model to the specific language and context of the task.

5.1.4 gbert-large (LM-finetuned)

The `gbert-large` model, finetuned with language model finetuning, achieved the best performance among all tested configurations. The final evaluation on the Competition test set, which included texts without labels, involved generating predictions using the ensemble models and submitting them for the GermEval contest. The final submission to the Closed Track achieved an average F1 score of 0.643 across all tasks, confirming the robustness of the finetuned `gbert-large` model.

The training procedure for the `deepset/gbert-large` model involved monitoring the training loss and validation F1 score across epochs to ensure proper convergence and avoid overfitting. Figure 3 shows the training loss and validation F1 score across 5 folds, providing insights into the training dynamics and model performance over time. The figure reveals that the training loss consistently decreases across all folds, indicating effective learning and reduction of error on the training data. Concurrently, the validation F1 score initially increases, reflecting improved model performance on the validation set. However, the validation F1 score plateaus after a few epochs, suggesting that further training does not significantly enhance validation performance and helps identify the point of diminishing returns.

5.2 Results of the Additional Experiments

5.2.1 german bert cased (task-finetuned on GAHD)

The `german bert cased` model, when task-finetuned on the filtered GAHD dataset, achieved an average F1 score of 0.5777. This performance did not surpass its LM-finetuned counterpart, indicating that additional task-specific finetuning with filtered data did not provide the expected benefits.

5.2.2 bert multilingual (task-finetuned on Danish)

The multilingual BERT model, after task-specific finetuning on Danish data (Zeinert et al., 2021), showed improved performance with an average F1 score of 0.5773. This improvement over the baseline multilingual model suggests that the model can adapt to new languages and transfer learning across them. However, it still did not outperform the German-specific models.

6 Discussion and Conclusion

This paper presents our approach to Shared Task 1 of the GermEval2024 GerMS-Detect competition (Subtask 1), focusing on predicting the severity of misogyny/sexism in text based on annotations from multiple human annotators. Our methodology primarily utilized a finetuned `deepset/gbert-large` model, which proved effective in understanding and detecting nuanced language features associated with misogyny and sexism.

Our ensemble approach, consisting of five `deepset/gbert-large` models each trained on a different fold of the dataset achieved an average F1 score of 0.643 across all tasks in the competition. Key to this success was the use of weighted loss functions to address class imbalance and an ensemble learning approach to enhance prediction robustness. Hyperparameter tuning using Optuna further optimized performance, ensuring the chosen hyperparameters were well-suited for the task (Akiba et al., 2019).

To explore cross-lingual transfer learning, we finetuned a multilingual BERT model on a Danish sexism dataset (Zeinert et al., 2021). While this model showed slight improvements in certain F1 scores after finetuning, it did not outperform

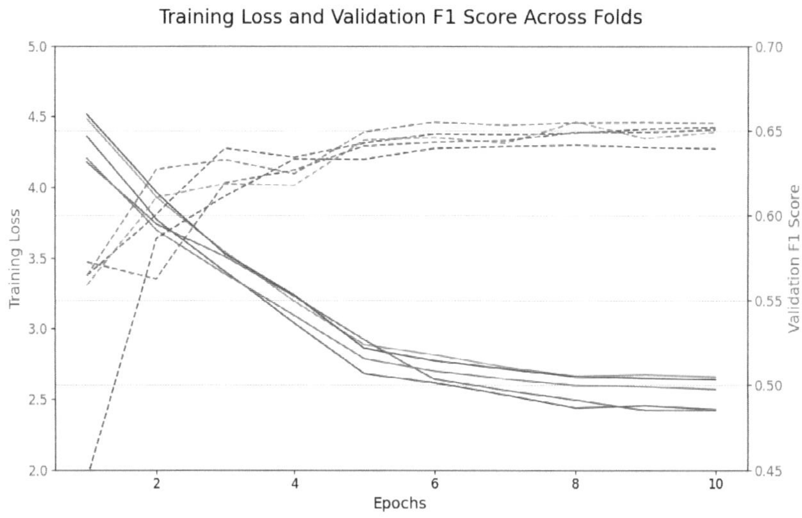

Figure 3: Training loss (solid lines) and validation F1 score (dashed lines) across epochs for 5 folds of the `gbert-large` model.

the standard `deepset/gbert-large` model. The marginal gains highlight the challenges inherent in cross-lingual transfer learning and the complexity of the task due to the subjective nature of the annotations.

We also investigated filtering the German adversarial hate speech dataset (GAHD) for misogynistic content using cosine similarity, aiming to improve the `german bert cased` model through additional pre-finetuning. This approach did not yield significant improvements, indicating that simply increasing misogynistic content in the training data is not sufficient to capture nuanced perceptions of sexism and misogyny, highlighting the complexity of developing effective models for detecting nuanced and subjective forms of hate speech (Fortuna and Nunes, 2018).

Our findings emphasize the importance of using specialized models tailored to specific linguistic contexts. Although the multilingual BERT model demonstrated some cross-lingual capabilities, the `deepset/gbert-large` model remained more effective for this task. Future research could explore more sophisticated methods for integrating multilingual data and better techniques for handling subjective annotations.

In summary, our work highlights the challenges and potential solutions for detecting misogyny and sexism in text. The advanced transformer models, ensemble learning, and careful handling of class imbalance were effective in achieving robust performance. However, the nuanced and subjective nature of this task requires further exploration and innovation to develop comprehensive and fair detection models.

Acknowledgements

This research was funded by the Bavarian State Ministry for Science and the Arts (StMWK: Bayerische Staatsministerium für Wissenschaft und Kunst - StMWK) as part of the Project "CHIASM" (Changenreiche industrielle Anwendungen für vortrainierte Sprachmodelle).

References

Takuya Akiba, Shotaro Sano, Toshihiko Yanase, Takeru Ohta, and Masanori Koyama. 2019. Optuna: A next-generation hyperparameter optimization framework. In *Proceedings of the 25th ACM SIGKDD International Conference on Knowledge Discovery & Data Mining*, KDD '19, pages 2623–2631, New York, NY, USA. Association for Computing Machinery.

Maria Anzovino, Elisabetta Fersini, and Paolo Rosso. 2018. Automatic identification and classification of misogynistic language on twitter. In *Natural Language Processing and Information Systems: 23rd International Conference on Applications of Natural Language to Information Systems, NLDB 2018, Paris, France, June 13-15, 2018, Proceedings 23*, pages 57–64. Springer.

Ayme Arango Monnar, Jorge Perez, Barbara Poblete, Magdalena Saldaña, and Valentina Proust. 2022. Resources for multilingual hate speech detection. In

Proceedings of the Sixth Workshop on Online Abuse and Harms (WOAH), pages 122–130.

Camiel J Beukeboom and Christian Burgers. 2019. How stereotypes are shared through language: a review and introduction of the aocial categories and stereotypes communication (SCSC) framework. *Review of Communication Research*, 7:1–37.

Branden Chan, Stefan Schweter, and Timo Möller. 2020. German's next language model. In *Proceedings of the 28th International Conference on Computational Linguistics*, pages 6788–6796, Barcelona, Spain (Online). International Committee on Computational Linguistics.

Jacob Devlin, Ming-Wei Chang, Kenton Lee, and Kristina Toutanova. 2019. BERT: Pre-training of deep bidirectional transformers for language understanding. In *Proceedings of the 2019 Conference of the North American Chapter of the Association for Computational Linguistics: Human Language Technologies, Volume 1 (Long and Short Papers)*, pages 4171–4186, Minneapolis, Minnesota. Association for Computational Linguistics.

Tracie Farrell, Miriam Fernandez, Jakub Novotny, and Harith Alani. 2019. Exploring misogyny across the manosphere in reddit. In *Proceedings of the 10th ACM conference on web science*, pages 87–96.

Paula Fortuna and Sérgio Nunes. 2018. A survey on automatic detection of hate speech in text. *ACM Comput. Surv.*, 51(4).

Anna Glazkova. 2023. A comparison of text preprocessing techniques for hate and offensive speech detection in twitter. *Social Network Analysis and Mining*, 13(1):155.

Janis Goldzycher, Paul Röttger, and Gerold Schneider. 2024. Improving adversarial data collection by supporting annotators: Lessons from GAHD, a German hate speech dataset. In *Proceedings of the 2024 Conference of the North American Chapter of the Association for Computational Linguistics: Human Language Technologies (Volume 1: Long Papers)*, pages 4405–4424, Mexico City, Mexico. Association for Computational Linguistics.

Ella Guest, Bertie Vidgen, Alexandros Mittos, Nishanth Sastry, Gareth Tyson, and Helen Margetts. 2021. An expert annotated dataset for the detection of online misogyny. In *Proceedings of the 16th Conference of the European Chapter of the Association for Computational Linguistics: Main Volume*, pages 1336–1350, Online. Association for Computational Linguistics.

Akshita Jha and Radhika Mamidi. 2017. When does a compliment become sexist? Analysis and classification of ambivalent sexism using Twitter data. In *Proceedings of the Second Workshop on NLP and Computational Social Science*, pages 7–16, Vancouver, Canada. Association for Computational Linguistics.

Amikul Kalra and Arkaitz Zubiaga. 2021. Sexism identification in tweets and gabs using deep neural networks. *Preprint*, arXiv:2111.03612.

Mladen Karan and Jan Šnajder. 2018. Cross-domain detection of abusive language online. In *Proceedings of the 2nd Workshop on Abusive Language Online (ALW2)*, pages 132–137, Brussels, Belgium. Association for Computational Linguistics.

Brigitte Krenn, Johann Petrak, Marina Kubina, and Christian Burger. 2024. GERMS-AT: A sexism/misogyny dataset of forum comments from an Austrian online newspaper. In *Proceedings of the 2024 Joint International Conference on Computational Linguistics, Language Resources and Evaluation (LREC-COLING 2024)*, pages 7728–7739, Torino, Italia. ELRA and ICCL.

Joseph Kwarteng, Serena Coppolino Perfumi, Tracie Farrell, Aisling Third, and Miriam Fernandez. 2022. Misogynoir: challenges in detecting intersectional hate. *Social Network Analysis and Mining*, 12(1):166.

Ilya Loshchilov and Frank Hutter. 2019. Decoupled weight decay regularization. *Preprint*, arXiv:1711.05101.

A.C. Mazari, N. Boudoukhani, and A. Djeffal. 2024. Bert-based ensemble learning for multi-aspect hate speech detection. *Cluster Computing*, 27:325–339.

Bonan Min, Hayley Ross, Elior Sulem, Amir Pouran Ben Veyseh, Thien Huu Nguyen, Oscar Sainz, Eneko Agirre, Ilana Heintz, and Dan Roth. 2023. Recent advances in natural language processing via large pre-trained language models: A survey. *ACM Comput. Surv.*, 56(2).

Benjamin Muller, Yanai Elazar, Benoît Sagot, and Djamé Seddah. 2021. First align, then predict: Understanding the cross-lingual ability of multilingual BERT. In *Proceedings of the 16th Conference of the European Chapter of the Association for Computational Linguistics: Main Volume*, pages 2214–2231, Online. Association for Computational Linguistics.

Karsten Müller and Carlo Schwarz. 2023. From hashtag to hate crime: Twitter and antiminority sentiment. *American Economic Journal: Applied Economics*, 15(3):270–312.

Debora Nozza, Claudia Volpetti, and Elisabetta Fersini. 2019. Unintended bias in misogyny detection. In *IEEE/WIC/ACM International Conference on Web Intelligence*, WI '19, pages 149–155, New York, NY, USA. Association for Computing Machinery.

Endang Wahyu Pamungkas, Valerio Basile, and Viviana Patti. 2020. Misogyny detection in twitter: a multilingual and cross-domain study. *Information Processing & Management*, 57(6):102360.

Fabio Poletto, Valerio Basile, Manuela Sanguinetti, Cristina Bosco, and Viviana Patti. 2021. Resources and benchmark corpora for hate speech detection: a systematic review. *Language Resources and Evaluation*, 55(3):477–523.

PyTorch Documentation. 2021. ReduceLROnPlateau.

Nils Reimers and Iryna Gurevych. 2019. Sentence-BERT: Sentence Embeddings using Siamese BERT-Networks. In *Proceedings of the 2019 Conference on Empirical Methods in Natural Language Processing*. Association for Computational Linguistics.

Julian Risch, Anke Stoll, Lena Wilms, and Michael Wiegand. 2021. Overview of the GermEval 2021 shared task on the identification of toxic, engaging, and fact-claiming comments. In *Proceedings of the GermEval 2021 Shared Task on the Identification of Toxic, Engaging, and Fact-Claiming Comments*, pages 1–12, Duesseldorf, Germany. Association for Computational Linguistics.

Phillip Rust, Jonas Pfeiffer, Ivan Vulić, Sebastian Ruder, and Iryna Gurevych. 2021. How good is your tokenizer? on the monolingual performance of multilingual language models. In *Proceedings of the 59th Annual Meeting of the Association for Computational Linguistics and the 11th International Joint Conference on Natural Language Processing (Volume 1: Long Papers)*, pages 3118–3135, Online. Association for Computational Linguistics.

Niloofar Safi Samghabadi, Parth Patwa, Srinivas PYKL, Prerana Mukherjee, Amitava Das, and Thamar Solorio. 2020. Aggression and misogyny detection using BERT: A multi-task approach. In *Proceedings of the Second Workshop on Trolling, Aggression and Cyberbullying*, pages 126–131, Marseille, France. European Language Resources Association (ELRA).

Marina Sokolova and Guy Lapalme. 2009. A systematic analysis of performance measures for classification tasks. *Information processing & management*, 45(4):427–437.

Lukas Stappen, Lea Schumann, Anton Batliner, and Bjorn W. Schuller. 2021. Embracing and exploiting annotator emotional subjectivity: An affective rater ensemble model. In *2021 9th International Conference on Affective Computing and Intelligent Interaction Workshops and Demos (ACIIW)*, pages 01–08.

Julia Maria Struß, Melanie Siegel, Josep Ruppenhofer, Michael Wiegand, and Manfred Klenner. 2019. Overview of GermEval Task 2, 2019 Shared Task on the Identification of Offensive Language. In *Proceedings of the 15th Conference on Natural Language Processing (KONVENS 2019)*, pages 354–365, Erlangen, Germany. German Society for Computational Linguistics & Language Technology.

Kathleen Van Royen, Karolien Poels, Heidi Vandebosch, and Philippe Adam. 2017. "Thinking before posting?" Reducing cyber harassment on social networking sites through a reflective message. *Computers in Human Behavior*, 66:345–352.

Michael Wiegand, Josef Ruppenhofer, and Thomas Kleinbauer. 2019. Detection of abusive language: the problem of biased datasets. In *Proceedings of the 2019 Conference of the North American Chapter of the Association for Computational Linguistics: Human Language Technologies, Volume 1 (Long and Short Papers)*, pages 602–608. Association for Computational Linguistics.

Michael Wiegand, Melanie Siegel, and Josef Ruppenhofer. 2018. Overview of the GermEval 2018 Shared Task on the Identification of Offensive Language. In *Proceedings of the 14th Conference on Natural Language Processing (KONVENS 2018)*.

Yousef Younes and Brigitte Mathiak. 2022. Handling class imbalance when detecting dataset mentions with pre-trained language models. In *Proceedings of the 5th International Conference on Natural Language and Speech Processing (ICNLSP 2022)*, pages 79–88.

Philine Zeinert, Nanna Inie, and Leon Derczynski. 2021. Annotating online misogyny. In *Proceedings of the 59th Annual Meeting of the Association for Computational Linguistics and the 11th International Joint Conference on Natural Language Processing (Volume 1: Long Papers)*, pages 3181–3197, Online. Association for Computational Linguistics.

FICODE at GermEval 2024 GerMS-Detect closed ST1 & ST2: Ensemble- and Transformer-Based Detection of Sexism and Misogyny in German Texts

Falk Maoro and **Michaela Geierhos**
University of the Bundeswehr Munich, Research Institute CODE
Werner-Heisenberg-Weg 39, Neubiberg, Germany
falk.maoro@unibw.de
michaela.geierhos@unibw.de

Abstract

In this paper, we present our solution for the shared task of GermEval 2024 GerMS-Detect. The joint task consists of two subtasks that we address in our solution. The texts in question may contain instances of sexism or misogyny and have been annotated in a multi-class classification setting. From this setting, two tasks are derived that require different binary or multi-class classifications. We propose an ensemble method using multiple sequence classification models that can be applied to both subtasks. With respect to **Subtask 1**, our approach achieves an average F1 score of **0.641**, and with respect to **Subtask 2**, our approach achieves an average Jensen-Shannon divergence of **0.354**. The code is available at the following link: https://github.com/fmaoro/germeval24

1 Introduction

The prevalence of sexism and misogyny in social media is a major concern. In order to address this issue, the GermEval 2024 GerMS-Detect shared task presents two subtasks on the identification of such misbehavior in German-language forum posts. We, the team *ficode*, propose a solution for the closed Subtask 1 and another solution for the closed Subtask 2. The shared task of GermEval 2024 GerMS-Detect provides German forum posts that have been annotated by multiple annotators to indicate the presence and strength of sexism and misogyny. Since there are multiple annotations per instance, the shared task focuses on predicting the distribution and further combined labels of the annotations. All required labels in both subtasks can be interpreted as sequence classification tasks.

Significant progress has been made in the area of language modeling tasks, such as sequence classification, with the advent of the transformer architecture proposed by Vaswani et al. (2017). In particular, Devlin et al. (2019) invented the Bidirectional Encoder Representations from Transformers (BERT), which represents an input sequence as an encoding that can be used to train multiple language modeling tasks. Since the BERT model was primarily trained on English data, the need for a German-specific BERT-like model was solved by GBERT (Chan et al., 2020). A powerful approach is needed to apply such BERT models because the tasks require a large number of predicted labels, and the classification of text into levels of sexism and misogyny is a rather complex task.

Ensemble learning, which integrates multiple models to achieve superior performance, is a robust approach to solving such complex machine learning tasks. Mohammed and Kora (2023) highlight the success of ensemble methods in various domains and their enhancement by deep learning models, despite the complexity of tuning such models. Kotary et al. (2023) introduce differentiable model selection, which optimizes ensemble composition by selecting the best performing models, thus overcoming the limitations of traditional methods. In addition, Wood et al. (2024) provide a unified theory of how model diversity reduces bias and variance, further improving ensemble performance. These works influence our approach to solving the two subtasks by highlighting the power of ensemble methods.

Therefore, we decided to use the pre-trained GBERT-large model as a baseline for fine-tuning with the available training data. The inherent German language knowledge of the model is advantageous for learning the nuances of sexism and misogyny in German texts. By training a total of six GBERT-based sequence classifiers and using them in an ensemble pipeline, we achieve an average F1 score of **0.641** for Subtask 1 and an average Jensen-Shannon divergence of **0.354** for Subtask 2.

The paper is organized as follows: Section 2 presents a brief analysis of the available training and test data. This includes an examination of the available labels and the distribution of annotations. Section 3 outlines the initial training approach. This serves as the basis for the predictions for the two subtasks. There is also a description of the methodology for using the models in an ensemble pipeline, followed by a description of the experimental setup in Section 4. An analysis of the results is presented in Section 5. Finally, Section 6 provides a concluding remark.

2 Data

The data consists of news forum posts labeled by multiple annotators. In the training subset, each post is assigned a unique ID, the text of the post itself, and a list of annotations. Each annotation contains a user pseudonym and one of the following labels: *0-Kein* (no sexism/misogyny), *1-Gering* (low sexism/misogyny), *2-Vorhanden* (present sexism/misogyny), *3-Stark* (strong sexism/misogyny), and *4-Extrem* (extreme sexism/misogyny).

In the test subset, each post is identified by a unique ID, accompanied by the text of the post and a list of the pseudonyms of the annotators who labeled the post. The training subset consists of 5,998 examples, while the test subset contains 1,986 examples. The number of annotations per example varies widely, ranging from 4 to 11 annotations. The average is 4.8 annotations per example.

Since there are multiple annotations per example, Subtask 1 defines a set of aggregating labels that need to be predicted. The first label is *bin_maj*, which is a boolean indicating that the majority of annotators assigned a label other than *0-Kein*. The label *bin_one* is also a boolean indicating that at least one annotator assigned a label other than *0-Kein*. The third binary label, *bin_all*, indicates that all annotators have assigned labels other than *0-Kein*. The only multi-class label is *multi_maj*, where the most common annotated label should be predicted. *disagree_bin* indicates if there is unanimous agreement on *0-Kein*.

The distribution of labels in Figure 1 and the distribution of labels for the class *multi_maj* in Figure 2 show a notable imbalance in all class labels, except for *bin_one*. Of particular interest is the low number of true *bin_all* labels compared to the number of positive labels. Furthermore, over 70 % of the annotated labels are *0-Kein*.

The analysis of the text data does not reveal any specific, conspicuous features. Table 1 shows the minimum, maximum and average number of characters, words, and tokens (tokenized with a

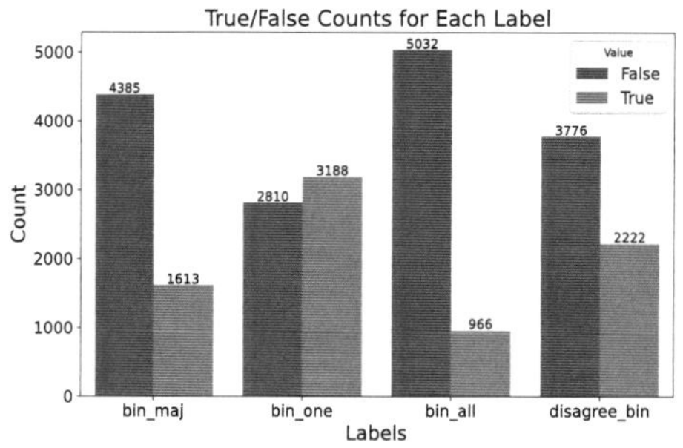

Figure 1: Label distribution for all binary labels.

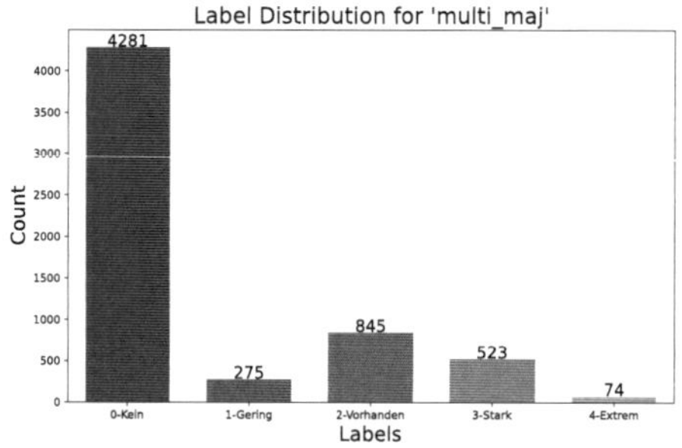

Figure 2: Label distribution for the class 'multi_maj'.

Variable	Minimum	Maximum	Mean
Characters	3	999	216.35
Words	1	173	32.87
Tokens	3	234	50.70

Table 1: Number of characters, words, and tokens for all training examples.

deepset/gbert-base tokenizer) for training subset examples. In addition, an examination of random samples revealed no need for preprocessing the input texts. Therefore, in our further work we use the input texts in their original form.

3 Concept

Our approach to solve the closed Subtask 1 and the closed Subtask 2 of the GermEval 2024 GerMS-Detect shared task is to train multiple BERT models for sequence classification. The models are first trained and then used for both tasks by post-processing their outputs in different ways. The models trained for the following subtasks are described in detail in Section 3.1. Then, in Section 3.2, we present the pipeline we used to solve Subtask 1. Finally, in Section 3.3, we describe our approach to solving Subtask 2.

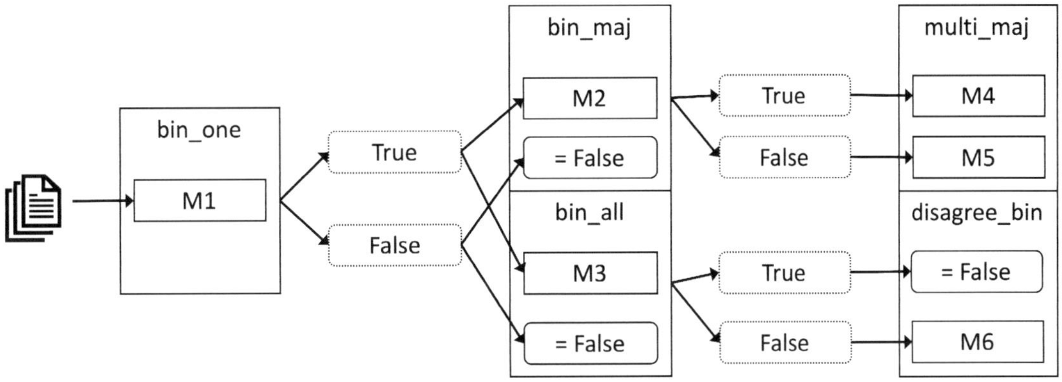

Figure 3: Pipeline for the closed Subtask 1.

3.1 Modeling

Since the subtasks require the prediction of five different binary and multi-class labels, we defined six different models.

The first model (**M1**) is a binary sequence classifier that receives all examples for training and predicts the label *bin_one*, which indicates whether there is at least one annotator who did not annotate *0-Kein*.

The second model (**M2**) receives all examples and classifies *bin_maj*. Therefore, the model has to predict whether there is a majority of annotators labeling other than *0-Kein*.

The third model (**M3**) is almost identical to **M2**, but differs in that it classifies *bin_all*, which indicates that all annotators labeled some form of sexism or misogyny.

The *multi_maj* classification is divided into two training sets. The fourth model (**M4**) is trained on examples that exhibit a clear form of sexism or misogyny, as indicated by the presence of at least one true instance of *bin_maj* or *bin_all*. In contrast, **M5** uses all available training examples to classify both distinct and indistinct examples.

The sixth model (**M6**) is applied to all examples where *bin_all* is not true and classifies *disagree_bin*.

3.2 Subtask 1

The approach for Subtask 1 uses the six models described in Section 3.1 in a sequential pipeline that is visualized in Figure 3. First, all examples in the test subset are predicted by **M1** to generate *bin_one* labels. Then, for all examples where the prediction of *bin_one* is true, **M2** predicts *bin_maj* and **M3** predicts *bin_all*. In cases where the prediction *bin_all* is true, the label *bin_maj* is also set to true. Conversely, if none of the labels are true or *bin_one* is false, both *bin_maj* and *bin_all* are set to false.

In all cases where the *bin_maj* prediction is true, **M4** predicts the *multi_maj* label. For all other examples, **M5** predicts the label *multi_maj*.

Finally, **M6** predicts the *disagree_bin* label for all instances where *bin_all* was predicted as false.

3.3 Subtask 2

Similar to our approach in Subtask 1, we use a pipeline to compute the required outputs. This pipeline is shown in Figure 4 and reuses a subset of the models from Subtask 1. Moreover, we do not extend the model training and we do not use the available data on the number of annotators per example in the training set.

For the *dist_bin* distribution, we need to predict the proportion of annotators who have labeled an example as *0-Kein* (not sexist) versus those who have labeled it as sexist or misogynist. Since our **M1** model has already been trained to predict whether there is at least one sexist vote for an example, it can be reused for this purpose. First, we take the example text and use the **M1** model to predict softmax values for both binary values (true and false). Then, instead of relying solely on the softmax scores to define the distribution, we use an algorithm that we call *Nearest Distribution Matcher*. The matcher first generates a list of evenly spaced numbers in the range of 0 to 1. The number of values in this list is equal to the sum of the number of annotators in the example plus 1. In the case of two annotators, the resulting list would contain the values [0, 0.5, 1], corresponding to 0 %, 50 %, and 100 %, respectively. The distribution is then computed using the value with the smallest difference to the softmax score for each label (true

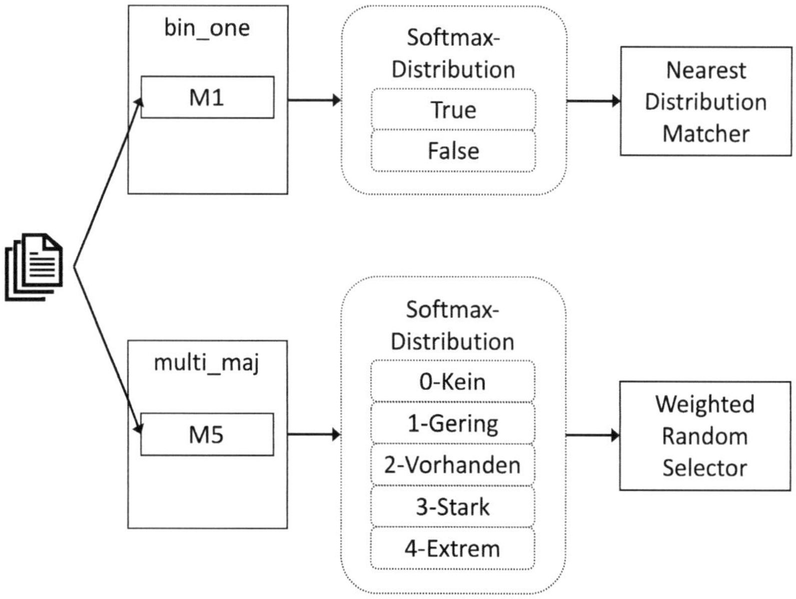

Figure 4: Pipeline for the closed Subtask 2.

and false).

The multi-score distribution, denoted *dist_multi*, is derived from the predictions of **M5**. Here we use the **M5** model to predict softmax scores for the example. To derive the distribution of annotated labels by the annotators, we use the softmax scores as probabilities for a *Weighted Random Selector*. For each annotator in the example, the selector chooses one of the five labels. Consequently, the final distribution is calculated by dividing the number of draws per label by the total number of draws for all labels in the example.

4 Training

Our training pipeline uses a pre-trained *deepset/gbert-large* model as a baseline for all six fine-tuned models. Therefore, for each task, a binary (**M1**, **M2**, **M3**, **M6**) or a multilabel (**M4**, **M5**) classification head with randomly initialized parameters is added to the encoder layer of the baseline model. For fine-tuning we use the raw texts of the training data and specify a learning rate between 2e-5 and 4e-5 and a number of epochs ranging from 8 to 30. We have manually tried to optimize the parameters in order to maximize the F1 score. The specific parameters for our models are available in the public repository[1].

In addition, the training pipeline uses all available training data for training, rather than splitting the data into training and validation subsets. We do this to maximize the number of training data points available for model training. Consequently, all models were first evaluated on the training set within the pipeline for the specific modeling tasks.

For fine-tuning our models and computing predictions, we utilized a system equipped with an NVIDIA A100 80GB PCIe GPU, supported by 128 GB of RAM and a 32-core Intel(R) Xeon(R) Gold 6248R CPU.

5 Results

After applying our ensemble method to the test data in Subtask 1, the predictions were uploaded to the shared task website for automated evaluation. The results for the five different classes and the final task score are shown in Table 2. Except for the labels *MultiMaj* and *DisagreeBin*, which achieved F1 scores of 0.414 and 0.610 respectively, all other labels achieved F1 scores of at least 0.7. This indicates that the challenging task was not unambiguous for the fine-tuned models. This may be due to the fact that the classification of text into levels of sexism or misogyny is sometimes a matter of interpretation, as even the annotators showed.

We also used the same trained models for Subtask 2, used them in the prediction pipeline for that task, and uploaded the predictions to the shared task website. The results are shown in Table 3. The results show that the distributions computed by our

[1] https://github.com/fmaoro/germeval24

Target Label	F1 Score
MultiMaj	0.414
BinMaj	0.744
BinOne	0.733
BinAll	0.705
DisagreeBin	0.610
Average Score	**0.641**

Table 2: Results for the closed Subtask 1.

pipeline have some differences, but still show substantial similarities to the distributions given by the annotated labels. Since our training process did not take into account the number of annotators or the distribution of labels, the result is rather weak. In addition, the randomness used for the weighted random selector affects each prediction, so running the pipeline again would produce different values.

In addition, the classification heads of the fine-tuned models were optimized to maximize the softmax scores for the true labels, and were not given any information about the distribution or uncertainty of the levels of sexism and misogyny.

Target Label	JS-Distance Score
Dist Multi	0.365
Dist Bin	0.343
Average Score	**0.354**

Table 3: Results for the closed Subtask 2.

6 Conclusion

In this work, we have proposed two related solutions for the two closed subtasks of the shared task GermEval 2024 GerMS-Detect. We solved the tasks by first training multiple BERT models to predict the labels of different subsets of the data. The use of six fine-tuned models (**M1–M6**) within a pipeline enabled strong performance for most of the classes in Subtask 1. The pipeline in Figure 3 was used to predict the labels of each example. Depending on the results of the first models, the further path in the pipeline was influenced. Thus, if an example was predicted to have no sexism / misogyny votes at all by the *binary_one* label, the further labels for *bin_all*, *bin_maj*, *multi_maj*, and *disagree_bin* were affected. This set of rules for applying models sequentially and only when necessary allowed for an efficient and effective use of the classifiers.

In addition, two of these models (**M1** and **M5**) were used to predict the distributions of annotators voting for the different labels in Subtask 2, with acceptable results. Using the softmax scores of the two classifiers in our Nearest Distribution Matcher and the Weighted Random Selector (see Figure 4), the distribution of annotators labeling the different levels was computed. Considering the uncertainty of classifying the level of sexism and misogyny in a text, the different results are understandable.

Acknowledgments

This work was funded by the German Federal Ministry of Education and Research under the grant no. 13N16242.

References

Branden Chan, Stefan Schweter, and Timo Möller. 2020. German's next language model. In *Proceedings of the 28th International Conference on Computational Linguistics*, pages 6788–6796, Barcelona, Spain (Online). International Committee on Computational Linguistics.

Jacob Devlin, Ming-Wei Chang, Kenton Lee, and Kristina Toutanova. 2019. BERT: Pre-training of deep bidirectional transformers for language understanding. In *Proceedings of the 2019 Conference of the North American Chapter of the Association for Computational Linguistics: Human Language Technologies, Volume 1 (Long and Short Papers)*, pages 4171–4186, Minneapolis, Minnesota. Association for Computational Linguistics.

James Kotary, Vincenzo Di Vito, and Ferdinando Fioretto. 2023. Differentiable model selection for ensemble learning. In *Proceedings of the Thirty-Second International Joint Conference on Artificial Intelligence, IJCAI-23*, pages 1954–1962. International Joint Conferences on Artificial Intelligence Organization. Main Track.

Ammar Mohammed and Rania Kora. 2023. A comprehensive review on ensemble deep learning: Opportunities and challenges. *Journal of King Saud University - Computer and Information Sciences*, 35(2):757–774.

Ashish Vaswani, Noam Shazeer, Niki Parmar, Jakob Uszkoreit, Llion Jones, Aidan N Gomez, Ł ukasz Kaiser, and Illia Polosukhin. 2017. Attention is all you need. In *Advances in Neural Information Processing Systems*, volume 30. Curran Associates, Inc.

Danny Wood, Tingting Mu, Andrew M. Webb, Henry W. J. Reeve, Mikel Luján, and Gavin Brown. 2024. A unified theory of diversity in ensemble learning. *J. Mach. Learn. Res.*, 24(1).

Team Quabynar at the GermEval 2024 Shared Task 1 GerMS-Detect (Subtasks 1 and 2) on Sexism Detection

Kwabena Odame Akomeah
University of Regensburg
kwabena-odame.akomeah@ur.de

Udo Kruschwitz
University of Regensburg
udo.kruschwitz@ur.de

Bernd Ludwig
University of Regensburg
bernd.ludwig@ur.de

Abstract

While large language models such as ChatGPT and GPT-3.5 Turbo offer impressive capabilities, their use can be costly and may not always be advisable, particularly for specific types of tasks. As part of our involvement in the GerMS-Detect challenge we observe that traditional, more cost-effective language models such as BERT are able to achieve better results than GPT-3.5 Turbo, a very robust LLM, when applied to sexist text classification. This suggests that for certain types of tasks and contexts, using BERT models may be a plausible alternative to state-of-the-art LLMs. This paper hightlights our approach to predicting annotator binary and soft labels using transformer models and an LLM in GermEval 2024 GerMS-Detect's open and closed subtasks of sexism detection.

1 Introduction

In an era where social media conversations and text proliferates exponentially (Guo et al., 2022), the need for vigilant moderation has gained much attention. As more people engage online, the challenge of identifying hate speech, toxic comments, and other harmful content has become increasingly urgent (Ayele et al., 2023). While much research has focused on English, the impact of harmful content extends beyond language barriers (Jahan and Oussalah, 2023). The link between hate speech and the spread of sexism is profound as the former can be explained in the later (Sen et al., 2022). Hate speech often perpetuates negative stereotypes and harmful ideologies, reinforcing societal norms that can lead to marginalization and oppression (Richardson-Self, 2021). This creates a feedback loop where sexist attitudes are normalized and disseminated through various channels, including social media, public discourse, and interpersonal interactions (Fox et al., 2015). The impact of this dynamic is far-reaching, influencing not only individual behaviors and beliefs but also institutional policies and cultural narratives (Richardson-Self, 2021). Understanding this connection is crucial for developing effective strategies to combat both hate speech and sexism, promoting a more inclusive and equitable society. Sexism can incite targeted hate or even violence against specific groups based on sex orientatation and identification (Sen et al., 2022). Thus, identifying content that warrants scrutiny is as crucial as identifying outright hate speech.

GermEval 2024 GerMS-Detect is part of a series of shared task evaluation campaigns that focus on Natural Language Processing (NLP) for the German language. This year's GerMS-Detect subtasks specifically target sexism detection in German online news fora, building upon previous years' efforts on detecting various texts with hate speech (Risch et al., 2021). GerMS-Detect goes beyond toxicity identification. It also delves into classifying annotated data by several annotators and combining them in different ensemble formats to attain both binary and soft labels aiming to foster healthier conversations online.

The goal of **subtask 1** was to predict labels for each text in a dataset, with these labels derived from the original annotations made by multiple human annotators. In contrast, **subtask 2** sought to predict the label distribution for each text in the same dataset, with this distribution based on the original allocation of labels predicted in subtask 1. These two subtasks were interrelated, as both aimed to accurately reflect the human annotators' evaluations, with subtask 1 focusing on discrete label prediction and subtask 2 on capturing the nuanced distribution of these labels.

Our participation in GermEval 2024 involved tackling two subtasks both in the closed and open competitions. Leveraging transformer-based model architectures from the huggingface repository, we specifically employed different BERT embeddings and finetuned with Pytorch for the closed competition and an LLM for the open competition. In the following sections, we will examine the dataset employed, discuss the selected model architectures in detail, and evaluate their performance on the designated subtasks. To support reproducibility the complete codebase for our experiments is available as a Github repository [1]

The dataset used in GerMS-Detect were delivered sequentially in 3 different sections namely the trial, development and competition phases where the later was a consolidation of all the dataset from the other two phases. The data used for training and testing with 5,998 labeled texts for training and 1,986 unlabeled for testing annotated by 10 human annotators sporadically. The distribution of annotations is uneven across the annotators. Three annotators (A002, A012, A010) have annotated all 5,998 texts, while others have annotated fewer, with the least being A001, who annotated 970 texts. Submissions were made on Codabench [2]

2 Model architectures

As set out in the shared task guidelines, our approach for the closed competition exclusively employed untrained transformer models that had not been exposed to any sexism or hate speech data. The models utilized in our study included Google's German BERT cased, multilingual BERT and Deepset's German BERT base.

General Approach. The data was loaded and preprocessed by aggregating all annotators into a unified dictionary of separate annotator dataframes. This new dataframe constituted the columns, ids, text and labels labels texts for each annotator in the dictionary. The initial data which was in JSON format had lists of annotators in one column and labels in another for each distinct id and text.

```
{'A001':
          id  \

0     a733e8a47708ce1d77060266d365e5b5
1     bf45fc2ac6742a7f75d5863c3338d59d
2     e1e80ff680f874d49ddfe33ac846a454
3     4689b9ccb5d79f222ba110f389cf1fb6
4     a8d04dfc8e63b67f4587b04524605e3e
..                                 ...
965   b13f0c202385d74b54f1fac4ea297510
966   f3bc2e041355ab9c1bba465a004f0631
967   841b039088a4edc7a14df7b231fd2f85
968   2414c1c9fd116539262aba5ee58de650
969   075cfd6f6dacfb11cc0a919bb21d70d2

      text
0     Wen man nicht reinläßt,...
1     Und eine Katze die schnurrt...
2     Des Oaschloch is eh scho ...
3     Trump hat 2 Dinge übersehen:...
4     Mit der Fox÷e hat er sich ...
..
965   was hat Zadic dazu veranlasst...
966                Uninteressant.
967   dem Islam die Frauenfeindl...
968   vielleicht spitzt sie jetzt...
969   Die Geschichte mit Astra...

     label  label_text
0      0       -Kein
1      0       -Kein
2      0       -Kein
3      0       -Kein
4      4     -Extrem
..
965    3      -Stark
966    0       -Kein
967    0       -Kein
968    0       -Kein
969    2  -Vorhanden
[970 rows x 4 columns],
'A002':
         id  \
0     a733e8a47708ce1d77060266d365e5b5
1     bf45fc2ac6742a7f75d5863c3338d59d
2     e1e80ff680f874d49ddfe33ac846a454
3     4689b9ccb5d79f222ba110f389cf1fb6
4     a8d04dfc8e63b67f4587b04524605e3e
...
      text
0     Wen man nicht reinläßt,...
1     Und eine Katze die schnurrt...
2     Des Oaschloch is eh scho ...
3     Trump hat 2 Dinge übersehen:...
4     Mit der Fox÷e hat er sich...

      label label_text
0        0      -Kein
1        0      -Kein
2        3     -Stark
3        3     -Stark
4        4    -Extrem
...
[5998 rows x 4 columns],
... }
```

Listing 1: A sample of the dictionary of annotator dataframes

Subsequently, the texts within the JSON file were regrouped by annotators and placed in container dataframes. The dataset was then partitioned into training and validation sets using a 90/10 percentage split for each annotator dataframe. This reason for ratio of 90:10 was ensure that majority of the dataset was included in the training rather than validation.

The dataset was then tokenized using the various BERT tokenizers implemented under the API Transformers and prepared for training with a batch

[1]https://github.com/kaodamie/Quabynar--GermDetect-2024

[2]https://www.codabench.org/competitions/

size of 16, a threshold that was appropriate for the GPU memory available. It is important to note that different BERT models have their corresponding tokenizers and it is advisable to stick to a matching tokenizer as this can affect training significantly. The BERT tokenizer is a tool that processes and converts input text into tokens, which are the basic units of text that the BERT model can use for various NLP tasks (Devlin et al., 2019). The BERT tokenizer is based on a specific tokenization technique called WordPiece (Devlin et al., 2019). Due to the training structure, which involved looping over several annotators, a significant amount of memory was required. With a GPU RAM of 12GB running PyTorch CUDA 12.0, the memory constraints were adequately managed.

Throughout the training process, metrics including accuracy, precision, recall, and F1 score were monitored and recorded for each iteration. The training loop was designed to iteratively adjust the model parameters, optimizing the learning rate and minimizing the loss function. Additionally, early stopping criteria with a patience of 3 epochs was implemented to prevent overfitting, ensuring the model maintained its generalization capability on the validation set and to save time taken to train the dataset. The model only stops and saves best weights when training metrics being tracked for each epoch does not improve after 3 additional epochs.

Post-training, the model's performance was evaluated using the unseen test data to confirm its robustness and reliability on codabench as per the regulations of the shared tasks. This was the only testing done due to the dataset size. Further splitting of the training dataset would have resulted in a smaller size for training that would have impacted the training results and model's capabilities. We observed that with this approach, testing results did what was achieved during training.

Subtask 1: Binary and Multi Labels Strategy

The objective of subtask 1 was to predict labels for each text in a dataset, where these labels are derived from those initially assigned by multiple annotators. The annotators, following certain annotation guidelines (Krenn et al., 2024), evaluated the presence and intensity of misogyny or sexism in the texts using the following labels:

- **0-Kein**: No sexism or misogyny present
- **1-Gering**: Mild sexism or misogyny
- **2-Vorhanden**: Sexism or misogyny present
- **3-Stark**: Strong sexism or misogyny
- **4-Extrem**: Extreme sexism or misogyny

Consequently, the degree of strength assigned to a text deemed sexist is largely subject to the annotator's personal judgment. Subtask 1 involved predicting labels based on various strategies for aggregating the multiple annotations into a single target label. The strategies are as follows:

- **bin_maj**: Predict 1 if the majority of annotators assigned a label other than 0-Kein. Predict 0 if the majority assigned a label of 0-Kein. If there is no clear majority, both labels 1 and 0 are accepted for evaluation.
- **bin_one**: Predict 1 if at least one annotator assigned a label other than 0-Kein, and 0 otherwise.
- **bin_all**: Predict 1 only if all annotators assigned labels other than 0-Kein, and 0 otherwise.
- **multi_maj**: Predict the majority label. If no majority label exists, any of the assigned labels are considered correct for evaluation.
- **disagree_bin**: Predict 1 if there is any disagreement among annotators and 0 otherwise.

The strategy for **multi_maj** was slightly modified to predict non-zero labels which was useful on the test data if there was no clear majority as follows: **multi_maj**: Predict the majority label. If no majority label exists, if non-zero labels exist, any of the assigned labels that are **non-zeros** are considered correct for evaluation otherwise predict zero. It was observed to be a more effective approach to attaining a much higher score on the leader-boards for both subtasks.

After this only text ids with the predictions of the test set were saved in .tsv format and uploaded for scoring.

Subtask 2: Predicting Annotator Distributions

For the subtask of predicting annotator distributions, only 2 runs were submitted to achieve a high score of 0.29 over the Shannon-Jensen evaluation of soft labels topping the leaderboard on subtask 2. The models employed in subtask 2 were Google's BERT mulitlingual cased and German BERT cased model. They were both fine-tuned over a GPU with a RAM of 12GB using PyTorch CUDA 12.0 with the same hyperperparameters discussed in subtask 1. In effect, the models were trained once for both subtasks and binary labels attained in subtask 1 were consequently converted to soft labels to fit subtask 2. Two types of distributions considered are binary score and multi-score distributions. Each set of distribution summed to 1.

- **dist_bin_0**: Represents the proportion of annotators who labeled the text as 'not-sexist' (0-Kein).
- **dist_bin_1**: Represents the proportion of annotators who labeled the text as 'sexist', which includes any of the labels 1-Gering, 2-Vorhanden, 3-Stark, or 4-Extrem.
- **dist_multi_0**: The proportion of annotators labeling the text as 0-Kein.
- **dist_multi_1**: The proportion of annotators labeling the text as 1-Gering.
- **dist_multi_2**: The proportion of annotators labeling the text as 2-Vorhanden.
- **dist_multi_3**: The proportion of annotators labeling the text as 3-Stark.
- **dist_multi_4**: The proportion of annotators labeling the text as 4-Extrem.

The strategy for prediction involved basing the distributions described above on the predicted binary labels from subtask 1 and applying the rules defined for substask 2 in subtask 2. This approach achieved a final score of 0.29 . See Table 2

All models were trained using the AdamW optimizer, initialized with the model's parameters and a learning rate of 2e-5. AdamW is a variant of the Adam optimizer that includes weight decay for better regularization. The loss was computed from the model's outputs. This loss quantifies how well the model's predictions match the target values. These were calculated over the accuracy of logits. Precision, recall and weighted F1 scores were carefully monitored per each epoch run for each model. The backward loss computed dloss/dx for every parameter x. These are accumulated into a gradient variable for every parameter x. The optimizer then updated the value of x using the gradient calculated above. This process was achieved by setting parameters using the "BertForSequenceClassification" definition in the transformer API. It was applied for each annotator in a loop, and the best weights were selected with early stopping over a total of 10 epochs, with a patience threshold of 3 epochs per annotator. See documentation at Huggingface.[3]

3 Open Subtask- Improving Training and Considerations for LLMs

The open competition was permitted for both subtasks 1 and 2 as specified in the terms and agreement of the competition. They allowed for models that had already been pretrained on sexism data and the use of additional dataset provided all information are open-source and results can be replicated. It was unrestricted and open to the use of models such as LLMs.

We applied few-shot learning on OpenAI's GPT 3.5 Turbo. We designed our model to select only the top 5 entries iteratively for each annotator. The model is also designed to preprocess a given text by truncating it to a specified length of 512 characters and then generate a short-length prediction using the GPT-3.5-turbo model with a 5 learning prompt. The truncate procedure ensures the input text remains within the length constraints, while a generate prediction function constructed an appropriate prompt and makes an API call to the language model to obtain a prediction. The parameters used were as follows:

Initialization. An instance of the OpenAI client is created using a provided API key. This client will be used to interact with the OpenAI API for generating text completions. Usage of OpenAI's models come at a cost based on the model and total tokens queried into the API.

Prompting. Prompting was conducted in English while instructing the LLM to analyze and respond to texts in German for the selected few-shot examples. The inclusion of the prompt message *"You are a helpful assistant."* in the API call serves to establish the context for the model, directing it to adopt a cooperative and helpful tone throughout the interaction.

This preliminary instruction is crucial as it sets

[3]`https://huggingface.co/transformers/v3.0.2/model_doc/bert.html`

Model	bin maj f1	bin one f1	bin all f1	multi maj f1	disagree bin f1	Final Score
BERT Multilingual Cased	0.6579	0.7158	0.5091	0.2393	0.6022	0.5448
German BERT Cased	0.6698	0.7344	0.6091	0.3423	0.6175	0.5946
German BERT Base	**0.6981**	**0.7290**	**0.6428**	**0.3706**	**0.6139**	**0.6109**
***GPT 3.5 Turbo**	*0.4751	*0.5586	*0.4849	*0.1967	*0.5455	*0.4522

Table 1: Subtask 1 Scores of Models. *Subtask 1 Open Results. Scores in green are our best scores attained for subtask 1

the expectation for the assistant's behavior, aiming to enhance the overall quality and relevance of the responses. By providing a clear and explicit directive on the assistant's role, the model is better positioned to deliver accurate, contextually appropriate, and user-friendly outputs, thereby improving the effectiveness of the interaction. This approach ensures that the assistant not only processes the given examples accurately but also maintains a consistent and supportive demeanor in its responses.

```
def generate_prediction(text,
    few_shot_prompt, max_tokens=50):
    text = truncate_text(text)  #
    Truncate the text to avoid exceeding
     the context length
    prompt = few_shot_prompt + f"Text: {
    text}\nLabel: "
    response = client.chat.completions.
    create(
        model="gpt-3.5-turbo",
        messages=[
            {"role": "system", "content"
    : "You are a helpful assistant."},
            {"role": "user", "content":
    prompt}
        ]
...

def format_few_shot_prompt(examples,
    max_examples=5):
    prompt ="The following texts are in
    German. Assign a label from 0 (not
    offensive) to 4 (most offensive):\n\
    n"
    for example in examples[:
    max_examples]:
        prompt += f"Text: {example['text
    ']}\nLabel: {example['label']}\n\n"
    return prompt
```

Listing 2: Code snippet

API Parameters. These parameters (max tokens as 50, n as 1 and a temperature of 0.3) are used in the API call to fine-tune the behavior and output of the model to best fit the task of classifying the offensiveness of the texts. By limiting the response to 50 tokens, we ensure that the output is concise and stays within a manageable length. This helps to control the cost and speed of the API call, as well as to avoid overly verbose answers. A lower temperature value (closer to 0) makes the output more deterministic and focused, while a higher value (closer to 1) makes it more random and creative. Setting the temperature to 0.3 made the model to provide more consistent and reliable predictions, which is generally suitable for tasks requiring accuracy. By setting n to 1, the function requests a single response from the model. This is useful for straightforward tasks where only one prediction is needed. If n were greater than 1, multiple responses would be generated, which could be useful for tasks requiring multiple perspectives or for ensemble methods.

Although the LLM's results were not actively explored by the team, there is room for much improvement in the technique by which training of the dataset was done. Selecting first 5 examples and sequentially prompting for each annotator in a loop may not necessarily ensure a balanced example text.

Effective prompting strategies and the inherent capabilities of large language models (LLMs) have in recent times been very popular in many different tasks and text generation (Liu et al., 2023). However, for this particular task, there are ways to further enhance the training process and considerations that need to be made regarding the use of LLMs in such future tasks in order to enhance results.

Annotated Data Quality. Ensuring that the data annotated by different users is of high quality and accurately represents the categories being predicted can significantly improve model performance (Li, 2024).

Data Diversity. Increasing the diversity of the training data by incorporating a wider range of examples from different contexts can help the model generalize better to unseen data (Chung et al., 2023). This includes expanding the dataset to cover various dialects, jargon, and situational contexts.

Contextual Prompts. Utilizing more sophisticated prompting techniques that provide better context and clearer instructions can help models like GPT-3.5 generate more accurate responses. Experimenting with different prompt formats and iteratively refining them based on feedback can lead to better outcomes (Zhou et al., 2023).

Hybrid Models. Exploring approaches that combine the strengths of different models, such as using BERT for initial feature extraction and GPT-3.5 Turbo for generating refined predictions, can leverage the advantages of each model type (Veeramani et al., 2024).

Ensemble Methods. Implementing ensemble methods that aggregate predictions from multiple models can enhance robustness and accuracy, particularly when dealing with complex or ambiguous inputs (García-Díaz et al., 2023).

4 Results

The results after prediction were put together indexing the ids of the various texting and joining the annotators and their corresponding predicitons in different sets over 2 columns. This new dataframe was saved as a compressed tsv file which was then submitted on Codabench. The performance of the system on all five predicted labels were evaluated using the F1 macro score across all classes before averaging the results as the final ranking. See Table 1.

The performance in subtask 2 were assessed using the Jensen-Shannon (JS) distance. This evaluation is applied to both the prediction of the binary distribution and the prediction of the multi-score distribution. The final score was determined by taking the unweighted average of the JS distances for both the binary and multi-score distribution predictions. See Table 2

For our final submission, the model fine-tuned on Deepset's German BERT base achieved a score of 0.61 on the test set for the binary subtask 1 (See Table 1) placing third whereas the model fine-tuned on Google's German BERT cased obtained a score of 0.29 over the Shannon-Jensen evaluation topping the leaderboard for subtask 2 on Codabench. See Table 2

Considering the results derived for the test set, the F1 scores for the multi majority were fairly low following an imbalance coverage in annotation by annotators. We believe much better metrics can be achieved given a much balanced dataset. This incomplete coverage suggests that some texts were annotated by only a subset of annotators, leading to potential biases or inconsistencies in the labeling process impacting model's training and testing, as the diversity of annotations for each text varies. These insights highlight the importance of analyzing annotator contributions and ensuring a fair and comprehensive annotation process for more robust ensemble model development in future.

5 Conclusion

While GPT-3.5 Turbo and similar LLMs have shown promise, particularly due to advancements in prompting and tokenization, it is crucial to evaluate their cost-effectiveness and suitability for specific tasks. BERT models, with their strong performance in this subtask, highlight the importance of selecting the right model based on task requirements. Future training improvements that focus on enhancing data quality, refining prompting strategies, optimizing tokenization, and exploring hybrid approaches through the implementation of ensemble methods that aggregate predictions from multiple models can potentially enhance robustness and accuracy, particularly when dealing with complex or ambiguous inputs. Ultimately, the choice of model should be guided by a careful assessment of the task at hand, resource availability, and the desired balance between performance and cost (Yang et al., 2024).

6 Future work

The findings from our current study emphasize several key areas for future work in leveraging large language models (LLMs) like GPT-3.5 Turbo and other top performing LLMs not mentioned in this study. Randomizing and balancing few-shot examples and comparing them accross various LLMs, adopting different fine-tuning approaches to few-shot and ensemble approaches with both LLMs and transformers are worth exploring. By addressing these areas, future work can build on the promising results of current LLMs, leading to more robust, accurate, and cost-effective applications in natural language processing and beyond.

References

Abinew Ali Ayele, Skadi Dinter, Seid Muhie Yimam, and Chris Biemann. 2023. Multilingual racial hate speech detection using transfer learning. In *Proceedings of the 14th International Conference on Recent Advances in Natural Language Processing*, pages

Model	JS Dist Bin	JS Dist Multi	Final Score
BERT Multilingual Cased	0.2646	0.3517	0.3081
German BERT Cased	0.2479	0.3361	0.2920
***GPT-3.5 Turbo**	*0.3661	*0.4521	*0.4091

Table 2: Subtask 2 Evaluation scores for different models. *Subtask 2 Open results. Scores in green are our best scores attained for subtask 2

41–48, Varna, Bulgaria. INCOMA Ltd., Shoumen, Bulgaria.

John Chung, Ece Kamar, and Saleema Amershi. 2023. Increasing diversity while maintaining accuracy: Text data generation with large language models and human interventions. In *Proceedings of the 61st Annual Meeting of the Association for Computational Linguistics (Volume 1: Long Papers)*, pages 575–593, Toronto, Canada. Association for Computational Linguistics.

Jacob Devlin, Ming-Wei Chang, Kenton Lee, and Kristina Toutanova. 2019. BERT: Pre-training of deep bidirectional transformers for language understanding. In *Proceedings of the 2019 Conference of the North American Chapter of the Association for Computational Linguistics: Human Language Technologies, Volume 1 (Long and Short Papers)*, pages 4171–4186, Minneapolis, Minnesota. Association for Computational Linguistics.

Jesse Fox, Carlos Cruz, and Ji Young Lee. 2015. Perpetuating online sexism offline: Anonymity, interactivity, and the effects of sexist hashtags on social media. *Computers in human behavior*, 52:436–442.

José Antonio García-Díaz, Camilo Caparros-laiz, Ángela Almela, Gema Alcaráz-Mármol, María José Marín-Pérez, and Rafael Valencia-García. 2023. UMUTeam at SemEval-2023 task 12: Ensemble learning of LLMs applied to sentiment analysis for low-resource African languages. In *Proceedings of the 17th International Workshop on Semantic Evaluation (SemEval-2023)*, pages 285–292, Toronto, Canada. Association for Computational Linguistics.

Zhijiang Guo, Michael Schlichtkrull, and Andreas Vlachos. 2022. A survey on automated fact-checking. *Transactions of the Association for Computational Linguistics*, 10:178–206.

Md Saroar Jahan and Mourad Oussalah. 2023. A systematic review of hate speech automatic detection using natural language processing. *Neurocomputing*, 546:126232.

Brigitte Krenn, Johann Petrak, Marina Kubina, and Christian Burger. 2024. GERMS-AT: A sexism/misogyny dataset of forum comments from an Austrian online newspaper. In *Proceedings of the 2024 Joint International Conference on Computational Linguistics, Language Resources and Evaluation (LREC-COLING 2024)*, pages 7728–7739, Torino, Italia. ELRA and ICCL.

Jiyi Li. 2024. A comparative study on annotation quality of crowdsourcing and llm via label aggregation. In *ICASSP 2024-2024 IEEE International Conference on Acoustics, Speech and Signal Processing (ICASSP)*, pages 6525–6529. IEEE.

Pengfei Liu, Weizhe Yuan, Jinlan Fu, Zhengbao Jiang, Hiroaki Hayashi, and Graham Neubig. 2023. Pre-train, prompt, and predict: A systematic survey of prompting methods in natural language processing. *ACM Computing Surveys*, 55(9):1–35.

Louise Richardson-Self. 2021. *Hate speech against women online: Concepts and countermeasures*. Rowman & Littlefield.

Julian Risch, Anke Stoll, Lena Wilms, and Michael Wiegand. 2021. Overview of the GermEval 2021 shared task on the identification of toxic, engaging, and fact-claiming comments. In *Proceedings of the GermEval 2021 Shared Task on the Identification of Toxic, Engaging, and Fact-Claiming Comments*, pages 1–12, Duesseldorf, Germany. Association for Computational Linguistics.

Indira Sen, Mattia Samory, Claudia Wagner, and Isabelle Augenstein. 2022. Counterfactually augmented data and unintended bias: The case of sexism and hate speech detection. In *Proceedings of the 2022 Conference of the North American Chapter of the Association for Computational Linguistics: Human Language Technologies*, pages 4716–4726, Seattle, United States. Association for Computational Linguistics.

Hariram Veeramani, Surendrabikram Thapa, and Usman Naseem. 2024. MLInitiative@WILDRE7: Hybrid approaches with large language models for enhanced sentiment analysis in code-switched and code-mixed texts. In *Proceedings of the 7th Workshop on Indian Language Data: Resources and Evaluation*, pages 66–72, Torino, Italia. ELRA and ICCL.

Jingfeng Yang, Hongye Jin, Ruixiang Tang, Xiaotian Han, Qizhang Feng, Haoming Jiang, Shaochen Zhong, Bing Yin, and Xia Hu. 2024. Harnessing the power of llms in practice: A survey on chatgpt and beyond. *ACM Trans. Knowl. Discov. Data*, 18(6).

Wenxuan Zhou, Sheng Zhang, Hoifung Poon, and Muhao Chen. 2023. Context-faithful prompting for large language models. In *Findings of the Association for Computational Linguistics: EMNLP 2023*, pages 14544–14556, Singapore. Association for Computational Linguistics.

Detecting Sexism in German Online Newspaper Comments with Open-Source Text Embeddings (Team GDA, GermEval2024 Shared Task 1: GerMS-Detect, Subtasks 1 and 2, Closed Track)

Florian Bremm[1], Patrick Gustav Blaneck[1], Tobias Bornheim[2], Niklas Grieger[1,3] and Stephan Bialonski[1,*]

[1]*Department of Medical Engineering and Technomathematics*
Institute for Data-Driven Technologies, FH Aachen University of Applied Sciences, Jülich, Germany
[*]*bialonski@fh-aachen.de*

[2]*ORDIX AG*

[3]*Department of Information and Computing Sciences, Utrecht University, Utrecht, The Netherlands*

Abstract

Sexism in online media comments is a pervasive challenge that often manifests subtly, complicating moderation efforts as interpretations of what constitutes sexism can vary among individuals. We study monolingual and multilingual open-source text embeddings to reliably detect sexism and misogyny in German-language online comments from an Austrian newspaper. We observed classifiers trained on text embeddings to mimic closely the individual judgements of human annotators. Our method showed robust performance in the *GermEval 2024 GerMS-Detect* Subtask 1 challenge, achieving an average macro F1 score of 0.597 (4th place, as reported on Codabench). It also accurately predicted the distribution of human annotations in GerMS-Detect Subtask 2, with an average Jensen-Shannon distance of 0.301 (2nd place). The computational efficiency of our approach suggests potential for scalable applications across various languages and linguistic contexts.

1 Introduction

The reliable detection of sexism and misogyny in online discussions has received increased attention in recent years (Fontanella et al., 2024). Since the events of "Gamergate" in August 2014 (Massanari, 2016), a harassment campaign targeting female journalists, research on sexism and misogyny in online platforms has gained momentum. Exposure to sexism can have tangible negative effects, for example discouraging women from participating in online discussions, as shown by an online survey conducted by an Austrian newspaper (Krenn et al., 2024). Given the often subtle and subjective nature of sexist content, moderators face significant challenges in identifying it. This highlights the need for effective detection tools that can support moderators creating more inclusive online spaces for women.

Previous efforts to automate the detection of sexism and misogyny have typically relied on machine learning methods, often treating sexism and misogyny as forms of hate speech (Jahan and Oussalah, 2023). Numerous datasets have been created to support the training and validation of general hate speech detection models (Poletto et al., 2021; Yu et al., 2024). More recently, specialized datasets aimed specifically at sexism or misogyny detection have been released for different languages, including English (Anzovino et al., 2018), Spanish (Rodríguez-Sanchez et al., 2020), and French (Chiril et al., 2020). Alongside these developments, several competitions, such as SemEval-2019 Task 5 (Basile et al., 2019), EXIST 2022 (Rodríguez-Sanchez et al., 2022), and SemEval-2023 Task 10 (Kirk et al., 2023), have been held to promote progress in identifying sexism and misogyny. However, German-language resources for sexism detection have been particularly limited (Yu et al., 2024). The introduction of GERMS-AT (Krenn et al., 2024), a dataset of about 8000 online comments of an Austrian newspaper annotated for sexist content, has significantly improved the prospects for developing and evaluating sexism detection models in German. This dataset includes diverse annotations from multiple individuals, capturing the variability in human judgment.

In this contribution, we study the ability of open-source text embedding models, i.e., the multilingual "mE5-large"[1] (Wang et al., 2024) and the monolingual "German BERT large paraphrase

[1]https://huggingface.co/intfloat/multilingual-e5-large

cosine"[2] model, to reliably detect sexism and misogyny in German-language online comments (GERMS-AT). Using these text embeddings, we observed that traditional machine learning classifiers, which are fast and inexpensive to train, robustly predict the judgments of human annotators. We detail our approach and describe the models that were evaluated in the *GermEval 2024 GerMS-Detect* shared tasks and the results we obtained on out-of-sample data. The implementation details of our experiments are available online[3].

2 Data and Tasks

2.1 Data

The dataset of the *GermEval 2024 GerMS-Detect* Shared Task consisted of 7984 German-language comments from the comment section of an Austrian online newspaper (Krenn et al., 2024). While all comments were in German, many comments contained Austrian dialects or slang (see Figure 1, Example 1).

Example 1:
"Des Oaschloch is eh scho berühmt, de virz'g Jungfrauen oide, notgeile Nonnen." (ID: `e1e80ff680f874d49ddfe33ac846a454`)
Trans.: "This asshole is already famous anyway, the forty virgins, old, horny nuns."

No. *0-absence*:	1	(A001)
No. *1-mild*:	0	
No. *2-present*:	1	(A007)
No. *3-strong*:	5	(A002, A003, A004, A005, A012)
No. *4-extreme*:	3	(A008, A009, A010)

Example 2:
"Warum wählen dann aber immer noch 36% der Frauen in Österreich die övp?" (ID: `0917bc805a3b4c3086ee7101f2740dad`)
Trans.: "Then why do 36% of women in Austria still vote for the ÖVP?"

No. *0-absence*:	4	(A002, A009, A010, A012)
No. *1-mild*:	0	
No. *2-present*:	0	
No. *3-strong*:	0	
No. *4-extreme*:	0	

Figure 1: Comments from the provided training dataset with annotations grouped by label (annotators shown in parentheses). The comment in *Example 1* contains an Austrian dialect and was annotated by all ten experts receiving a variety of labels. *Example 2* was only annotated by four experts and received the same label from all of them.

Each comment was annotated by at least four annotators out of a group of ten human experts following specific guidelines[4]. Annotators were asked to label each comment as either not-sexist (0) or sexist (1–4). If a comment was identified as sexist, annotators assigned a label between 1 and 4, indicating the severity of the sexism or misogyny (1-mild, 2-present, 3-strong, 4-extreme). The annotations were highly subjective and varied significantly between annotators (see Figure 1). Figure 2 illustrates this variability in the annotations and highlights the imbalance in the number of comments labeled by each annotator. Additionally, Figure 2 shows, that the distribution of the five labels is highly imbalanced, with the majority of comments being labeled as not-sexist (0) by all annotators.

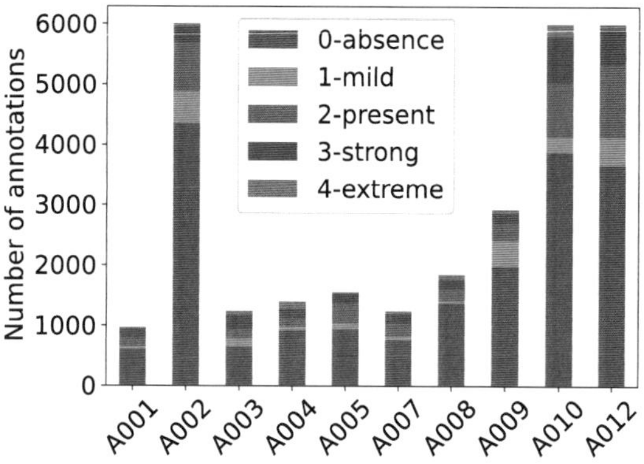

Figure 2: Distribution of the labels assigned by each annotator (A001–A012). Note that there are no annotations from users A006 and A011.

For the final phase of the Shared Task, the organizers provided a training dataset containing 5998 comments (75.1%) and a test dataset containing 1986 comments (24.9%), which was used for the evaluation of the final models on the competition website. The test dataset did not contain any annotations, but included the IDs of the annotators who labeled each comment. We employed two different data splits for model exploration and final training, respectively. During model exploration, we randomly split the provided training dataset into a smaller training set with 80% of the comments and a validation set containing the remaining 20%. We then created annotator-specific training sets by filtering the reduced training set for the annotations of each annotator. Furthermore, each annotator-specific training set was split into five folds for a cross-validation setup. For final training, we used the entire provided training set and, similar to the

[2] `https://huggingface.co/deutsche-telekom/gbert-large-paraphrase-cosine`
[3] `https://github.com/dslaborg/germeval2024`
[4] `https://ofai.github.io/GermEval2024-GerMS/guidelines.html` (Krenn et al., 2024)

model exploration phase, created annotator-specific training sets with 10% of the data reserved for early stopping.

2.2 Tasks

The Shared Task consisted of two subtasks. In *Subtask 1*, all annotations of a comment were aggregated into a single prediction target using various strategies. The goal was then to predict the aggregated label of each aggregation strategy for each comment. The following aggregation strategies were used:

- *Majority (binary prediction target)*: A comment is labeled as *not-sexist* or *sexist* depending on whether the majority of annotators labeled the comment as not-sexist (0) or sexist (1–4). If there is no majority, both labels are considered valid. In Figure 1, *Example 1* would be labeled as *sexist* and *Example 2* as *not-sexist*.

- *One (binary)*: If at least one annotator labeled a comment as sexist (1–4), the comment is labeled as *sexist*, otherwise as *not-sexist*. In Figure 1, *Example 1* would be labeled as *sexist* and *Example 2* as *not-sexist*.

- *All (binary)*: If all annotators labeled a comment as sexist (1–4), the comment is labeled as *sexist*, otherwise as *not-sexist*. In Figure 1, both examples would be labeled as *not-sexist*.

- *Majority (multi-class)*: The label of a comment is the majority label of all annotators for this comment. If there is no majority, each of the labels assigned by the annotators is considered valid. In Figure 1, *Example 1* would be labeled as *3-strong* and *Example 2* as *0-absence*.

- *Disagreement (binary)*: If at least one annotator labeled a comment as sexist (1–4), while at least one other annotator labeled the same comment as not-sexist (0), the comment is labeled as *disagreed*. Otherwise, the comment is labeled as *agreed*. In Figure 1, *Example 1* would be labeled as *disagreed* and *Example 2* as *agreed*.

In contrast to the binary and multi-class targets of *Subtask 1*, the goal of *Subtask 2* was to model the relative distribution of annotations per comment. The following two distributions were of interest:

- *Binary*: The portion of annotators labelling a comment as *not-sexist* (0) or *sexist* (1–4) respectively. In Figure 1, *Example 1* would be labeled as 10% *not-sexist* and 90% *sexist*. *Example 2* would be labeled as 100% not-sexist.

- *Multi-Class*: Each prediction target represents the portion of annotators labelling a comment as one of the five labels (0–4). In Figure 1, *Example 1* would be labeled as 10% *0-absence*, 0% *1-mild*, 10% *2-present*, 50% *3-strong*, and 30% *4-extreme*. *Example 2* would be labeled as 100% *0-absence*.

3 Methods and Results

Both subtasks of the *GermEval 2024 GerMS-Detect* Shared Task required knowledge of the distribution of annotations per comment. Since the test dataset contained information about the annotators that labeled the comments, we decided to train individual models for each annotator. In our approach, we combined pre-trained open-source large language models for text embeddings with simple classifiers to predict the annotations of an annotator.

3.1 Model Architecture

All comments were embedded into high-dimensional vector spaces using either (i) the "German BERT large paraphrase cosine" (GBERT-large-pc) model[5], a version of the monolingual German-BERT model (Chan et al., 2020) that was fine-tuned for text embeddings by Deutsche Telekom or (ii) the multilingual "mE5-base"[6] or "mE5-large"[7] (Wang et al., 2024) models. A general overview of the models used for text embeddings is provided in Table 1.

Model	Layers	Embedding Size
mE5-base	12	768
mE5-large	24	1024
GBERT-large-pc	24	1024

Table 1: Overview of the models used for text embeddings. The models were used as is, without any further fine-tuning.

[5] https://huggingface.co/deutsche-telekom/gbert-large-paraphrase-cosine

[6] https://huggingface.co/intfloat/multilingual-e5-base

[7] https://huggingface.co/intfloat/multilingual-e5-large

Hyperparameter	Value/Range
Multilayer Perceptron	
hidden_layer_sizes	$[64, 2048]$
class_weight	oversampled
Random Forest	
n_estimators	$[10, 560]$
criterion	gini
max_depth	$[1, 91]$
class_weight	balanced
Support Vector Machine	
C	$[1, 91]$
kernel	rbf
class_weight	balanced

Table 2: Overview of the hyperparameter ranges used for tuning the classifiers. The hyperparameters were explored using grid search with 5-fold cross-validation. The hyperparameter "class_weight" indicates how the class imbalance was addressed.

The resulting text embeddings were then used as input features for each of the following classifiers: (i) Multilayer Perceptron (MLP), (ii) Random Forest (RFC), and (iii) Support Vector Machine (SVC).

3.2 Model Training and Evaluation

Model training consisted of a model exploration phase, where we optimized hyperparameters and selected the best-performing classifier, and the final training, where we retrained the optimal training configurations on the entire training set for submission to the competition. During training, only the classifier was updated, while the text embeddings were kept fixed. When training the Multilayer Perceptrons, we used 10% of the training data as an early stopping set to prevent overfitting.

We optimized hyperparameters separately for each annotator and classifier type using 5-fold cross-validation on each annotator's training dataset (see Section 2.1 for details on the data split). Table 2 provides an overview of the hyperparameters of each classifier and their search ranges that were explored using grid search. To mitigate the class imbalance in the dataset (see Section 2.1), we balanced the classes for each annotator-specific dataset by either using class weights (preferred) or oversampling, depending on the respective model implementation by scikit-learn[8] (see Table 2).

After hyperparameter tuning, we retrained models for each annotator in the best-performing configuration on the entire annotator-specific training set and evaluated them on the validation set to identify the best-performing classifier type. For evaluation, we aggregated the predictions of each annotator's model using the respective aggregation strategies for Subtasks 1 and 2 (see Section 2.2). We then evaluated the performance of the aggregations using the Macro-F1 score for Subtask 1 and the Jensen-Shannon distance (Lin, 1991) for Subtask 2.

Once the best-performing classifier was identified, we recombined the training and validation sets and retrained the models on the entire dataset for each annotator. The final models then predicted the annotations of the test set, which were aggregated for Subtasks 1 and 2 using the same strategies as during model exploration and submitted to the competition.

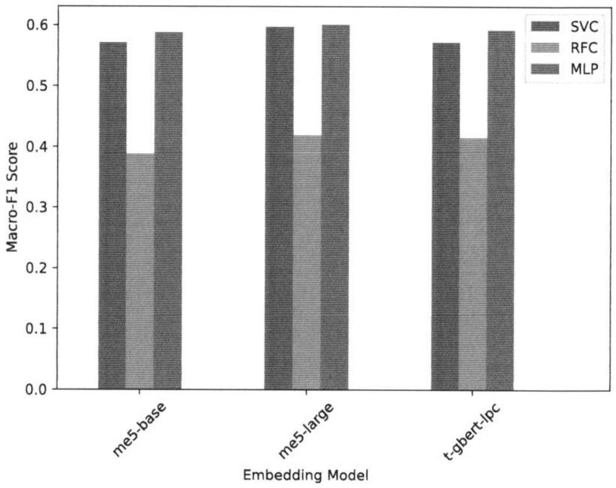

Figure 3: Macro-F1 scores our models achieved when aggregating the predictions for Subtask 1 on the validation set (higher is better).

3.3 Results

Figures 3 and 4 show the performance of our models on the validation set at the end of the model exploration phase for Subtask 1 and Subtask 2, respectively. The Multilayer Perceptron and the Support Vector Machine achieved similar scores on both subtasks, with the MLP performing slightly better on Subtask 1 and the SVC on Subtask 2 for all text embedding models. In comparison, the Random Forest classifier performed worse on average on both subtasks. While model performance did not vary significantly between the different text embedding models, the mE5-large embeddings consistently outperformed the mE5-base embeddings.

[8] https://scikit-learn.org/stable/

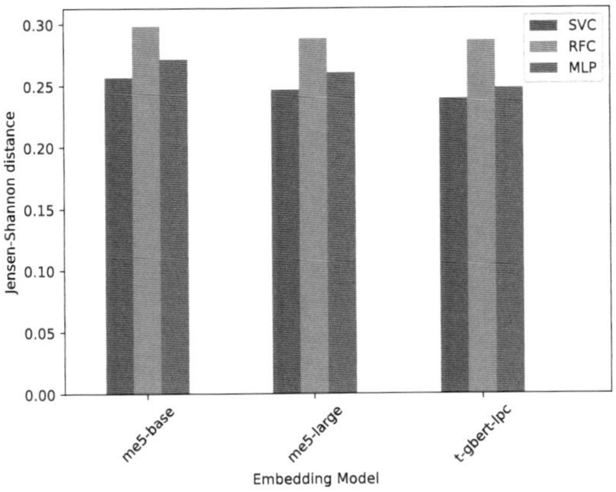

Figure 4: Jensen-Shannon distances our models achieved when aggregating the predictions for Subtask 2 on the validation set (lower is better).

The embeddings from the GBERT-large-pc model performed slightly worse than the mE5-large embeddings on Subtask 1 but achieved slightly better results on Subtask 2.

Accordingly, we decided to submit variations of the Multilayer Perceptron and the Support Vector Machine classifiers with mE5-large and GBERT-large-pc embeddings to the competition. Our best-performing model for Subtask 1 was the Support Vector Machine classifier on top of mE5-large embeddings with a Macro-F1 score of 0.597, ranking 4th on the Codabench leaderboard. For Subtask 2, the Support Vector Machine classifier with GBERT-large-pc embeddings achieved the best results with an average Jensen-Shannon distance of 0.301, ranking 2nd on the leaderboard.

4 Conclusion

Our study demonstrates that support vector machines trained on open-source text embeddings can robustly predict sexism and misogyny in German-language online comments, reflecting the diversity of human judgments. While the efficiency and low cost of our training process is an advantage of our approach, we see potential for further improvements. For example, jointly fine-tuning text embeddings and classifiers on sexism datasets could improve performance, as demonstrated by the top system in the EXIST 2022 challenge, which excelled at detecting sexism in Twitter tweets (Serrano, 2022). In addition, creating ensembles of fine-tuned text embedding models and classifiers could also lead to better results, similar to the strategy employed by the winning system in the GermEval 2021 challenge for identifying toxic Facebook comments (Bornheim et al., 2021). We foresee that advanced sexism detection systems can greatly assist social media moderators, paving the way for more respectful and inclusive online interactions in the future.

Acknowledgements

We are grateful to M. Reißel and V. Sander for providing us with computing resources.

References

Maria Anzovino, Elisabetta Fersini, and Paolo Rosso. 2018. *Automatic Identification and Classification of Misogynistic Language on Twitter*, page 57–64. Springer International Publishing.

Valerio Basile, Cristina Bosco, Elisabetta Fersini, Debora Nozza, Viviana Patti, Francisco Manuel Rangel Pardo, Paolo Rosso, and Manuela Sanguinetti. 2019. SemEval-2019 task 5: Multilingual detection of hate speech against immigrants and women in Twitter. In *Proc. 13th Int. Workshop on Semantic Evaluation*, pages 54–63, Minneapolis, Minnesota, USA. Association for Computational Linguistics.

Tobias Bornheim, Niklas Grieger, and Stephan Bialonski. 2021. FHAC at GermEval 2021: Identifying german toxic, engaging, and fact-claiming comments with ensemble learning. *CoRR*, abs/2109.03094.

Branden Chan, Stefan Schweter, and Timo Möller. 2020. German's next language model. In *Proc. 28th Int. Conf. on Computational Linguistics, COLING 2020*, pages 6788–6796, Barcelona, Spain (Online). International Committee on Computational Linguistics.

Patricia Chiril, Véronique Moriceau, Farah Benamara, Alda Mari, Gloria Origgi, and Marlène Coulomb-Gully. 2020. An annotated corpus for sexism detection in french tweets. In *Proc. 12th Language Resources and Evaluation Conf., LREC 2020*, pages 1397–1403, Marseille, France. European Language Resources Association.

Lara Fontanella, Berta Chulvi, Elisa Ignazzi, Annalina Sarra, and Alice Tontodimamma. 2024. How do we study misogyny in the digital age? A systematic literature review using a computational linguistic approach. *Humanities and Social Sciences Communications*, 11(1).

Md Saroar Jahan and Mourad Oussalah. 2023. A systematic review of hate speech automatic detection using Natural Language Processing. *Neurocomputing*, 546:126232.

Hannah Kirk, Wenjie Yin, Bertie Vidgen, and Paul Röttger. 2023. Semeval-2023 Task 10: Explainable detection of online sexism. In *Proc. 17th Int. Workshop on Semantic Evaluation, SemEval@ACL 2023*, pages 2193–2210. Association for Computational Linguistics.

Brigitte Krenn, Johann Petrak, Marina Kubina, and Christian Burger. 2024. GERMS-AT: A sexism/misogyny dataset of forum comments from an austrian online newspaper. In *Proc. Joint Int. Conf. on Computational Linguistics, Language Resources and Evaluation, LREC/COLING 2024*, pages 7728–7739. ELRA and ICCL.

Jianhua Lin. 1991. Divergence measures based on the shannon entropy. *IEEE Trans. Inf. Theory*, 37(1):145–151.

Adrienne Massanari. 2016. #Gamergate and The Fappening: How reddit's algorithm, governance, and culture support toxic technocultures. *New Media Soc.*, 19(3):329–346.

Fabio Poletto, Valerio Basile, Manuela Sanguinetti, Cristina Bosco, and Viviana Patti. 2021. Resources and benchmark corpora for hate speech detection: A systematic review. *Lang. Resour. Eval.*, 55(2):477–523.

Francisco J. Rodríguez-Sanchez, Jorge Carrillo-de-Albornoz, and Laura Plaza. 2020. Automatic classification of sexism in social networks: An empirical study on twitter data. *IEEE Access*, 8:219563–219576.

Francisco J. Rodríguez-Sanchez, Jorge Carrillo-de-Albornoz, Laura Plaza, Adrián Mendieta-Aragón, Guillermo Marco Remón, Maryna Makeienko, María Plaza, Julio Gonzalo, Damiano Spina, and Paolo Rosso. 2022. Overview of EXIST 2022: sexism identification in social networks. *Proces. del Leng. Natural*, 69:229–240.

Alejandro Vaca Serrano. 2022. Detecting and classifying sexism by ensembling transformers models. In *Proc. Iberian Languages Evaluation Forum (IberLEF 2022) co-located with the Conf. Spanish Society for Natural Language Processing (SEPLN 2022)*, volume 3202 of *CEUR Workshop Proceedings*. CEUR-WS.org.

Liang Wang, Nan Yang, Xiaolong Huang, Linjun Yang, Rangan Majumder, and Furu Wei. 2024. Multilingual E5 text embeddings: A technical report. *CoRR*, abs/2402.05672.

Zehui Yu, Indira Sen, Dennis Assenmacher, Mattia Samory, Leon Fröhling, Christina Dahn, Debora Nozza, and Claudia Wagner. 2024. The unseen targets of hate - A systematic review of hateful communication datasets. *CoRR*, abs/2405.08562.

pd2904 at GermEval2024 (Shared Task 1: GerMS-Detect): Exploring the Effectiveness of Multi-Task Transformers vs. Traditional Models for Sexism Detection (Closed Tracks of Subtasks 1 and 2)

Pia Donabauer
Information Science
University of Regensburg
pia.donabauer@stud.uni-regensburg.de

Abstract

The rise of social platforms has led to an increase in hateful, racist and sexist comments, impacting mental health and well-being. Detecting sexist texts automatically is a crucial first step to addressing this issue. This paper describes two approaches for the GermEval2024 GerMS-Detect Shared Task 1 on identifying sexist and misogynistic multi-annotated comments. Given the challenge of imbalanced data, the effectiveness of a multi-task transformer BERT model with TF-IDF weights is compared against traditional machine learning models. After training each model with individually optimized hyperparameters, 5-fold cross-validation showed that the traditional approach appears to perform better than the transformer model in several metrics. Given these results, the solution based on traditional models was submitted, achieving an F_1 score of 0.483 for subtask 1 and a Jensen-Shannon distance of 0.338 for subtask 2 in the final submission. The code is publicly available on GitHub [1].

1 Introduction

Although the rapid development of technology and social network sites has facilitated global communication, the anonymity online has enabled the unpunished expression of hateful, racist and sexist discourses (Rodríguez-Sánchez et al., 2020). This leads users to engage in behaviours they would avoid in face-to-face interactions, known as the *online disinhibition effect* (Wright et al., 2019). As a result, insults and harassment, such as sexism and misogyny, are prevalent in social media and online fora. Sexism is defined as prejudice, stereotyping, or discrimination based on sex, while misogyny refers to the hatred or dislike of women (Rodríguez-Sánchez et al., 2020). The variety and volume of language used in online platforms make it challenging to manage these issues (Bellmore et al., 2015). As victims of online sexist insults suffer from low self-esteem, emotional distress, and other negative emotions (Felmlee et al., 2020), it is crucial to develop language-specific models for sexism detection to foster a safer online environment. Given this real-world problem, GermEval2024 GerMS-Detect aims to identify sexism and misogyny in German-language comments from an Austrian online newspaper. The texts have been labeled by multiple human annotators, often with differing opinions. The submissions described in this paper are limited to the competition's closed track, which prohibits the use of additional data labeled for sexism, models or embeddings trained on data labeled for sexism, and Large Language Models (LLMs). This constraint requires the exploration of alternative solutions. Therefore, this paper elaborates on two approaches for detecting sexism in online fora: 1) several conventional machine learning classifiers, including Random Forest, Extreme Gradient Boosting (XGBoost), Light Gradient-Boosting (LightGBM), Support Vector Machines (SVM), and CatBoost, and 2) a deep learning transformer-based method, specifically a multi-task model using Bidirectional Encoder Representations from Transformers (Devlin et al., 2018) (BERT) with the integration of term frequency–inverse document frequency (TF-IDF). Multiple traditional models are experimented with, as performance across tasks may differ (Panwar and Mamidi, 2023). Evaluation shows that while the transformer-based approach yields promising results, hyperparameter-tuned conventional models tailored to each annotator turn out to perform better on predicting sexism in these experiments. This paper describes the implemented models for the GermEval2024 shared task, discusses possible reasons for the performance differences, and highlights the importance of developing effective detection methods to mitigate sexism and misogyny in online spaces.

[1] https://github.com/piadonabauer/GermEval2024

2 Background

GermEval2024's shared task focuses on detecting sexism and misogyny in texts posted in German-language to the comment section of an Austrian online newspaper.

2.1 Task Description

The shared task is divided into two subtasks:

Subtask 1: Predict a binary label indicating the presence or absence of sexism in four different ways, based on the original grading of the texts by several annotators; also predict the majority grading assigned by annotators. Evaluation is based on the macro-averaged F_1 score.

Subtask 2: Predict binary soft labels, based on the different opinions of annotators about the text; predict the distribution of the original gradings by annotators. Evaluation uses Jensen-Shannon distance to compare predicted and actual distributions.

Both subtasks are organized into closed tracks, where only the provided dataset may be used and advanced approaches such as LLMs are prohibited, and open tracks, where all materials and methods are allowed. Participation in this paper is limited to the closed track.

2.2 Annotations

The dataset is annotated by a varying subset of ten annotators using numeric classes ranging from 0 to 4, with 0 = not sexist, 1 = mildly sexist, 2 = sexist, 3 = strongly sexist, and 4 = extremely sexist. However, while the annotation guidelines[2] define what types of sexism and misogyny should be annotated, there are no rules about the severity, resulting in annotations reflecting personal judgments.

2.3 Dataset Exploration

GermEval 2024's labeled dataset in German-language consists of 5998 entries, with an unlabeled dataset of 1986 entries for competition submission. One data example, along with its annotations, is displayed in Table 1.

Corpus statistics show variation in the length of data points, ranging from 1 to 173 words. On average, each data point contains approximately 32.9 words, with a median length of 23.0 words. Figure 1 and Figure 2 provide insights into the distributions of annotators and labels. The imbalance in label distribution is apparent, with label 0 (non-sexist) being the most prevalent category. In Figure 1, the leftmost red bar represents 65% of all data points, indicating missing annotations, as not every annotator labeled every data point. Additionally, a few annotators made limited contributions by providing fewer than 2000 annotations, as shown in Figure 2.

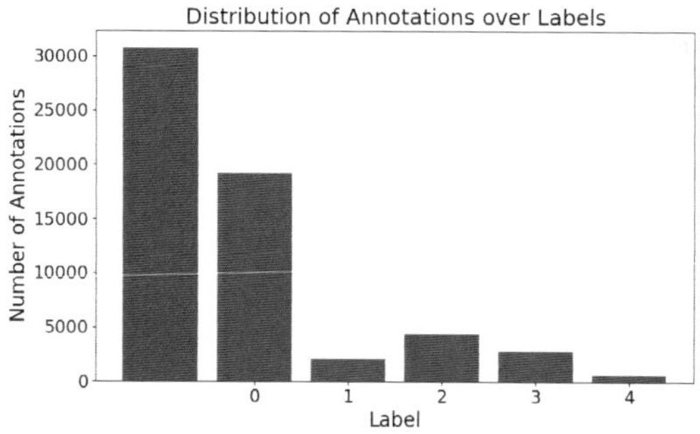

Figure 1: Distribution of labels given by all annotators collectively. The red bar visualizes missing annotations, since not all annotators labeled every data point.

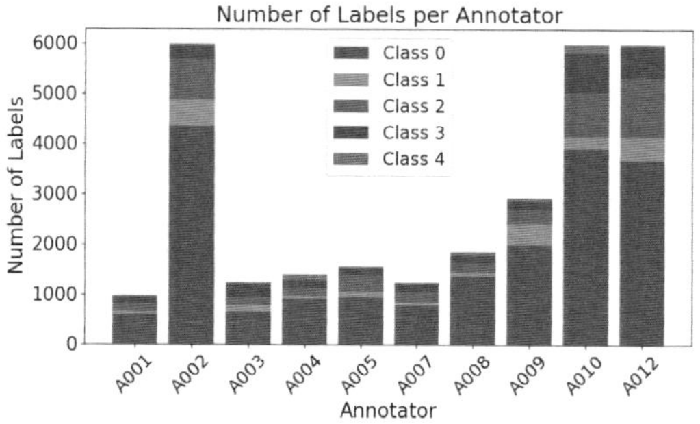

Figure 2: Distribution of labels given by each annotator individually.

Lastly, pairwise agreement among annotators was assessed using Krippendorff's Alpha. The highest agreement between two annotators was 0.043, suggesting highly diverse labeling strategies. Therefore, clustering annotators based on their agreements was not feasible.

3 Related Work

Extensive research has been conducted in the field of sexism prediction, multi-task frameworks, and data augmentation. Therefore, this section will primarily focus on recent concepts closely related to the competition.

[2] https://ofai.github.io/GermEval2024-GerMS/guidelines.html

German	Mit der Fox÷e [sic] hat er sich keinen Gefallen getan. Ja, ich weiß der Ausdruck ist eigentlich nicht forums tauglich.
English	He didn't do himself any favours with that cx÷t [sic]. Yes, I know the expression is not really suitable for a forum.

Annotations

Annotator ID	01	02	03	04	05	07	08	09	10	12
Label	4	4	4	4	3	4	2	3	4	2

Table 1: An example comment in German and English-language with its corresponding labels.

3.1 Multi-Task Learning

Advances in deep neural networks have enabled multi-task models to learn multiple tasks simultaneously, sharing parameters across tasks to improve training efficiency and performance (Xu et al., 2022). Zhou (Zhou, 2023) used multi-task learning to approach the hierarchical classification of sexism by pre-training RoBERTa and DeBERTa models on 2 million data points, resulting in boosted performance of their models. In other works, multi-task models were used to address the issue of disagreement among annotators for multi-labeled text. Davani et al. (Davani et al., 2022) proposed a multi-annotator architecture in order to preserve the internal consistency of each annotator's labels. Their multi-task model includes a fully connected layer explicitly fine-tuned for each annotator, predicting each annotator's judgments as separate subtasks after being trained on 27k and 50k data points, respectively.

3.2 Data Augmentation

Augmenting new data is the synthesis of existing training data, aiming to improve the performance of a downstream model (Wong et al., 2016). Due to participating in the closed track, the focus of this work will be on traditional augmentation methods (Schmidhuber and Kruschwitz, 2024). For instance, Butt et al. (Butt et al., 2021) applied *Back Translation* for data augmentation using the *deep-translator* library. By translating Spanish and English data into German and then back to their respective languages, the identification of sexism could be enhanced. Furthermore, to address the issue of class imbalance within their dataset, Martinez et al. (Martinez et al., 2023) employed *Random Oversampling* to replicate minority classes with slight variations. Other research applied multiple strategies (Mohammadi et al., 2023), such as performing *Synonym Replacement*, the replacement of words with their synonyms, *Random Word Swapping*, randomly swapping pairs of words in the text, and *Random Character Insertion*, randomly inserting characters into words.

3.3 Summary

Drawing inspiration from these studies, the approach in this work adopts a multi-task learning framework inspired by Zhou's model (Zhou, 2023), where the different tasks correspond to the different subtasks of the competition, but with fewer data points. The multi-annotator architecture proposed by Davani et al. (Davani et al., 2022) is integrated, leveraging the sharing of knowledge in initial layers to enhance generalization. Additionally, data augmentation methods are employed, specifically *Back Translation* and *Synonym Replacement* inspired by previous research, as augmentation has shown performance improvements. This combined approach is designed to take advantage of the strengths of these previous models.

4 Experimental Setup

As annotator disagreement may capture important nuances, all annotators' judgements were treated as separate tasks within the multi-annotator architecture. The described approach encompassed two main strategies: a multi-task transformer fine-tuning framework, where each task corresponds to predicting labels from individual annotators, and a baseline comparison involving the individual training of conventional machine learning models tailored to each annotator.

To optimize model performance, a hierarchical classification was adopted, initially predicting binary labels followed by multi-class prediction on texts categorized as sexist.

4.1 Materials & Methods

Due to significant imbalance in label distribution, methods for data balancing[3] were explored, such as the integration of class weights for each annotator's labels, and implementation of Focal Loss. The latter approach incorporates disagreement among annotators into the loss function during training, inspired by Plank et al. (Plank et al., 2014). While in these experiments class weights enhanced model performance, utilizing Focal Loss did not yield improved results in this setting, thus it was not employed.

Further experimentation involved feature engineering of text vectorization, incorporating lexical features, and testing various transformer models. Preprocessing steps such as lemmatization, stemming, and stop word removal harmed model performance, confirming previous work (Xu, 2022), hence the data was preserved in its original form.

In order to address the little amount of data to train a transformer model with multiple heads, especially since the number of data points for some annotators was less than 2000, data augmentation was performed. Additionally, the training of the conventional models benefited from the availability of more data. The intention of augmenting data was not to improve class balance, thus downsampling of most frequent classes was not performed.

Data Augmentation

The provided dataset was expanded from 5998 to 17'913 entries using two augmentation techniques, namely *Back Translation* and *Synonym Replacement*, which were mainly found in recent works (Butt et al., 2021; Mohammadi et al., 2023).

- **Back Translation**: Utilizing Helsinki NLP models (de-en[4] and en-de[5]), sentences were translated to English and then back-translated to German. Duplicates resulting from translations were removed.

- **Synonym Replacement**: Replacing tokens with synonyms using vectors for the German language from fasttext[6], filtering synonyms based on original POS tags. The words *woman*, *women*, *man* and *men* were kept for contextual relevance.

Example augmentations for both techniques are displayed in Table 2.

4.2 Classification Models

For model training, the shuffled dataset was split into a training (85%, N=15'226) and testing split (15%, N=2'687). Other than the methods described, we did not apply any techniques to account for class, annotator, or augmented data balance. Final model training was performed on 100% of the data. The code was developed using the PyTorch framework.

4.2.1 Transformer for Multi-Task Learning

Despite having less training data for transformers compared to previous research, BERT was fine-tuned for multi-task classification, expecting this approach to benefit from sharing knowledge among layers and thus enhancing robustness and generalization (Hashimoto et al., 2016; Davani et al., 2022).

Architecture: Training on various transformer architectures, such as *bert-base-german-cased*[7], *bert-base-multilingual-cased*[8] and *xlm-roberta-large-finetuned-conll03-german*[9] from HuggingFace, resulted in *bert-base-german-cased* showing the best performance as the backbone. The model architecture of BERT was modified to process CLS token embeddings through newly introduced shared dense layers, facilitating dimensionality reduction and feature extraction via ReLU activations, dropout regularization (0.2), and batch normalization. Following the implementation of ten annotator-specific output heads, utilizing sigmoid activation for binary tasks and softmax for multi-class tasks, TF-IDF scores were integrated. Inspired by Chen et al. (Chen et al., 2020), during the forward pass, the CLS token output from BERT was multiplied by TF-IDF weights specific to the training data, which were precomputed and stored in dictionaries. This approach allows the model to benefit from BERT's contextual embeddings and the importance of individual terms as captured by

[3] https://datascientest.com/en/management-of-unbalanced-classification-problems-ii

[4] https://huggingface.co/Helsinki-NLP/opus-mt-de-en

[5] https://huggingface.co/Helsinki-NLP/opus-mt-en-de

[6] https://fasttext.cc/docs/en/crawl-vectors.html

[7] https://huggingface.co/google-bert/bert-base-german-cased

[8] https://huggingface.co/google-bert/bert-base-multilingual-cased

[9] https://huggingface.co/FacebookAI/xlm-roberta-large-finetuned-conll03-german

Back Translation	German	English
Original	"Ich **habe wahnsinnige** Kopfschmerzen!" Mädchen - neue generation - Angst vor **eh** fast allem....	"I **have** a **terrible** headache!" Girls - new generation - afraid of almost everything...
Augmented	"Ich **hatte verrückte** Kopfschmerzen!" Mädchen - neue Generation - Angst vor fast allem **sowieso**...	"I **had** a **crazy** headache!" Girls - new generation - afraid of almost everything **anyway**...
Synonym Replacement	**German**	**English**
Original	Das **schöne Gesicht der** Frauenquote	The **beautiful face** of the women's quota
Augmented	Das **wunderschöne Antlitz die** Frauenquote	The **wonderful countenance** of the women's quota

Table 2: Examples of comments in their original form and their variations through the data augmentation techniques of *Back Translation* and *Synonym Replacement*.

TF-IDF. The loss function accounts only for available labels provided by annotators, ignoring any missing values.

Training: The multi-task learning approach uses a shared BERT backbone and dense layers trained collectively across all tasks. Each annotator has a specific output head for predicting their annotations, trained simultaneously. Loss is calculated separately for each annotator's head using the appropriate loss function. The total loss for each training step is the sum of the losses from all heads, used to update both the shared BERT backbone and annotator-specific heads.

Hyperparameter tuning was conducted to identify optimal values, including the learning rates and number of epochs. Stochastic Gradient Descent optimization with 10% warm-up steps, a cosine weight decay of 1e-4, a batch size of 16, and a maximum sequence length of 64 was used. For binary classification, the tuning process determined a learning rate of 5e-3 for 6 epochs, while for multi-task classification, it identified a learning rate of 1e-2 for 7 epochs.

Feature Engineering: Beyond TF-IDF scores, additional features (e.g. sentiment analysis, token length, and punctuation ratios) did not improve performance and were therefore excluded from the final solution.

4.2.2 Conventional Machine Learning Models

The baseline comparison involves an intuitive approach for multi-annotator models, where several conventional classifiers are trained, each one individually on the labels provided by a single annotator. Given performance variations among models in sexism detection observed by Panwar et al. (Panwar and Mamidi, 2023), multiple traditional model architectures including Random Forest, SVM, XGBoost, LightGBM, and CatBoost were explored. Hyperparameter tuning and feature engineering using CountVectorizer, TfidfVectorizer, and transformer methods were conducted for each annotator, with training enhanced by class weights.

5 Results

During training of the traditional models for binary prediction, the choice of model for each annotator was varied with all models (Random Forest, LightGBM, XGBoost, SVM, and CatBoost) being employed. The most frequently used one was XGBoost, selected four out of ten times. Vectorization using the *bert-based-german-cased* model showed the best results seven out of ten times. For multi-class labeling, only the models Random Forest, XGBoost, and LightGBM were deployed, with Random Forest and XGBoost being the most common, each selected four out of ten times. The vectorization techniques used most frequently this time were both Transformer and CountVectorizer, each used four out of ten times. Detailed assignments and hyperparameter tuning results can be found in the code.

Due to time constraints, model evaluation was based on accuracy, precision, recall, and F_1 score, rather than using the specified evaluation metrics for the subtasks. Both the BERT model and conventional models were evaluated on the test split after each training epoch and separately using 5-fold cross-validation, as shown in Table 3. For the traditional approach, an individual model was trained for each annotator, hence evaluation results were averaged across all ten models for both binary and multi-class classifications. The displayed metrics are solely for performance evaluation and do not refer to any submitted outcome. Evaluation results on the test split indicate that the BERT model seems to perform better than traditional models in binary classification. However, in multi-class classification, the performance is more variable, with traditional models achieving higher accuracy and F_1 scores. When assessed using 5-fold cross-validation, traditional models consistently perform better than BERT across most metrics for both classification tasks, except in binary classification where BERT shows higher precision.

Final submission results show that the traditional models achieved a lower Jensen-Shannon distance and thus better values compared to BERT, as visualized in Table 5. Therefore, the traditional models were chosen as the final submission approach for subtasks 1 and 2, resulting in the metrics shown in Tables 4 and 5. Details of the evaluation of the submission can be found on the original competition website for subtasks 1[10] and 2[11].

6 Discussion

This section elaborates on two multi-annotator frameworks designed to predict individual labels corresponding to different annotators.

6.1 Model Architectures

The baseline approach showed that hyperparameter tuning played a crucial role in optimizing model performance, with diverse model selection underscoring a rigorous approach to achieving the best results. Especially XGBoost proved to be a suitable choice due to its effective handling of sparse data. Its ability to automatically learn imputation strategies and its incorporation of L1 and L2 regularization techniques help prevent overfitting by penalizing complex models (Nielsen, 2016). These attributes may have contributed to XGBoost being the top-performing traditional model in this multi-annotator scenario.

The multi-task approach initially demonstrated promising results on the 15% test split. TF-IDF scores emphasized term importance, while additional features such as sentiment analysis, token length, or punctuation ratios did not enhance performance, possibly due to the model's difficulty in extracting meaningful patterns. However, during 5-fold cross-validation, traditional models showed better performance in all metrics except for precision in binary classification. Given that these findings contrast with previous research, such as the work by Davani et al. (Davani et al., 2022), which reported that the multi-task architecture obtained better results than the baseline models, possible reasons for this outcome are discussed.

6.2 Occurrence of Overfitting

To evaluate potential overfitting in the multi-task model, training loss and accuracy were plotted, as shown in Figure 3. For binary classification, loss steadily decreased and accuracy increased, but training was stopped after 7 epochs due to stagnation in evaluation metrics. For multi-class classification, training continued beyond optimal performance, achieving minimal loss and maximum accuracy after 4 epochs. This suggests a high likelihood of overfitting, particularly in the multi-class setting. This unintended overfitting is further observed in 5-fold cross-validation, which shows worse performance compared to the test split evaluation, likely due to the model's overfitting to the training data and resulting in less generalizable performance across different splits.

6.3 Data Augmentation and Leakage

The initial assumption that general data augmentation would be the most effective strategy led to neglecting the downsampling of frequently occurring classes, which might have improved performance. Furthermore, augmenting data, shuffling, and then splitting it into training and test sets caused data leakage. This overlap of transformed data points between training and testing phases led to misleadingly high performance metrics on the test set, as the model encountered familiar data points during testing. This increased the chances of overfitting and may explain the discrepancy between high evaluation results and lower final submission scores. This issue affects both models.

Furthermore, the distribution of annotations,

[10] https://ofai.github.io/GermEval2024-GerMS/subtask1.html
[11] https://ofai.github.io/GermEval2024-GerMS/subtask2.html

Model Evaluation	Metric	Binary		Multi-class	
		Test Split	5-fold CV	Test Split	5-fold CV
Multi-task BERT + TF-IDF	Accuracy	**0.807**	0.659	0.445	0.247
	Precision	**0.818**	**0.830**	**0.762**	0.446
	Recall	**0.796**	0.549	**0.540**	0.494
	F_1	**0.750**	0.661	0.337	0.470
Traditional ML Models	Accuracy	0.737	**0.768**	**0.561**	**0.586**
	Precision	0.782	0.780	0.738	**0.640**
	Recall	0.628	**0.768**	0.474	**0.586**
	F_1	0.690	**0.742**	**0.559**	**0.546**

Table 3: Evaluation results on the test split (15%) and 5-fold cross-validation after training both the fine-tuned multi-task BERT and the traditional models. For the traditional models, metrics from all ten models tailored to individual annotators were averaged, each for binary and multi-class classification. Predictions were made using a hierarchical approach, starting with binary and followed by multi-class predictions.

Subtask 1	
Model	**Traditional ML**
bin_maj_f1	0.543
bin_one_f1	0.633
bin_all_f1	0.458
multi_maj_f1	0.223
disagree_bin_f1	0.560
Total Score	**0.483**

Table 4: The final submission scores for subtask 1 are measured using F_1 scores. Specifically: **bin_maj** represents if most annotators' label are non-zero; **bin_one** indicates if any annotator labeled it as non-zero; **bin_all** shows if all annotators label it as non-zero; **multi_maj** refers to the majority label; **disagree_bin** captures cases where there is disagreement among annotators on zero versus non-zero labels. The final score is the unweighted average of these five F_1 scores. Given that traditional models showed better results in subtask 2, only this approach was submitted for subtask 1.

Subtask 2		
Model	**MT BERT**	**Trad. ML**
js_dist_bin	0.433	**0.306**
js_dist_multi	0.540	**0.371**
Total Score	0.487	**0.338**

Table 5: The final submission scores for subtask 2 are measured using the Jensen-Shannon Distance. Here, **dist_bin_0** refers to the portion of annotators labeling the text as 'not-sexist', while **dist_bin_1** refers to the portion of annotators labeling the text as 'sexist'. Lower scores indicate smaller distances and thus better performance. The final score is the unweighted average of the two distances.

classes, and other factors was not consistent across training and test sets, potentially leading to unbalanced data and performance issues during training and thus harming performance.

6.4 Dataset Size and Model Complexity

Despite the benefits of data augmentation, tripling the dataset size may still have been insufficient for fine-tuning ten separate heads in a transformer model, particularly due to the limited number of sexist instances for each annotator. Traditional models, which require less data, demonstrated better performance, likely due to their better feature representation handling in multi-class tasks with numerous annotators and skewed label distributions.

The performance decrease of the multi-task model could also be related to the choice of backbone architecture. To keep the approach simple, only BERT was used. Future research should explore enhanced versions such as RoBERTa and DistilBERT trained for the German language, as they may be crucial for performance improvement.

Ethical Statement: The annotated dataset from the GermEval2024 competition, gathered in accordance with ethical standards, was used. The dataset contained sexist remarks, posing risks to those targeted. The described classification algorithms were designed not to exacerbate harm; they address online sexism and foster inclusivity and equity. This

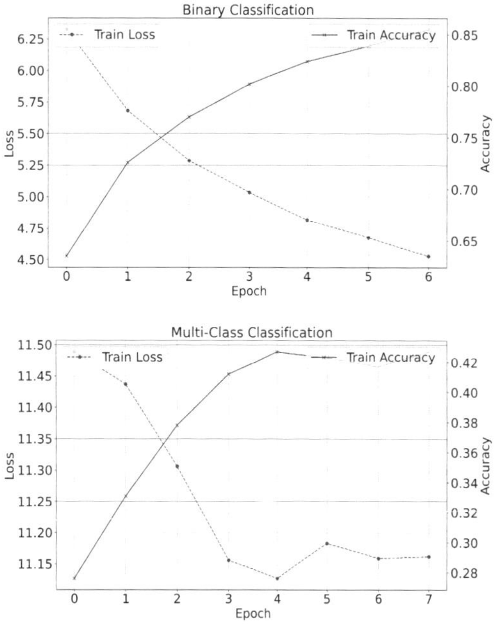

Figure 3: Plotted accuracy (blue) and loss (red) during training of the multi-task transformer for binary and multi-class classification.

study aims to contribute to automated technologies for analyzing sexism, enhancing awareness to combat oppression. This work represents a modest step towards a more equitable online environment.

7 Conclusion

This paper presents different multi-annotator methods for detecting sexism and misogyny in German-language comments, addressing challenges arising from a highly imbalanced dataset and diverse annotations provided by ten annotators. The study evaluates the effectiveness of two primary approaches: conventional machine learning models and a multi-task transformer with BERT architecture. Extensive experiments with various feature combinations and hyperparameter tuning were conducted. Results demonstrate that hyperparameter-tuned traditional models achieved better performance metrics than the multi-task transformer in detecting sexism. Furthermore, the importance of ensuring a consistent distribution of annotations and classes across dataset splits and avoiding data leakage by augmenting only the training data is emphasized. These findings highlight the difficulty of achieving reliable results in multi-task learning with limited data, especially in contexts where annotator opinions vary widely. Future research should validate these observations and explore new methods for multi-task learning frameworks, as well as hybrid models that leverage the strengths of both traditional and deep learning approaches.

References

Amy Bellmore, Angela J Calvin, Jun-Ming Xu, and Xiaojin Zhu. 2015. The five w's of "bullying" on twitter: Who, what, why, where, and when. *Computers in human behavior*, 44:305–314.

Sabur Butt, Noman Ashraf, Grigori Sidorov, and Alexander F Gelbukh. 2021. Sexism identification using bert and data augmentation-exist2021. In *IberLEF@ SEPLN*, pages 381–389.

Weilong Chen, Xin Yuan, Sai Zhang, Jiehui Wu, Yanru Zhang, and Yan Wang. 2020. Ferryman at semeval-2020 task 3: bert with tfidf-weighting for predicting the effect of context in word similarity. In *Proceedings of the fourteenth workshop on semantic evaluation*, pages 281–285.

Aida Mostafazadeh Davani, Mark Díaz, and Vinodkumar Prabhakaran. 2022. Dealing with disagreements: Looking beyond the majority vote in subjective annotations. *Transactions of the Association for Computational Linguistics*, 10:92–110.

Jacob Devlin, Ming-Wei Chang, Kenton Lee, and Kristina Toutanova. 2018. Bert: Pre-training of deep bidirectional transformers for language understanding. *arXiv preprint arXiv:1810.04805*.

Diane Felmlee, Paulina Inara Rodis, and Amy Zhang. 2020. Sexist slurs: Reinforcing feminine stereotypes online. *Sex roles*, 83(1):16–28.

Kazuma Hashimoto, Caiming Xiong, Yoshimasa Tsuruoka, and Richard Socher. 2016. A joint many-task model: Growing a neural network for multiple nlp tasks. *arXiv preprint arXiv:1611.01587*.

Elizabeth Martinez, Juan Cuadrado, Juan Carlos Martinez-Santos, and Edwin Puertas. 2023. Detection of online sexism using lexical features and transformer. In *2023 IEEE Colombian Caribbean Conference (C3)*, pages 1–5. IEEE.

Hadi Mohammadi, Anastasia Giachanou, Ayoub Bagheri, et al. 2023. Towards robust online sexism detection: a multi-model approach with bert, xlm-roberta, and distilbert for exist 2023 tasks. In *Working Notes of the Conference and Labs of the Evaluation Forum (CLEF 2023)*, volume 3497, pages 1000–1011. CEUR Workshop Proceedings.

Didrik Nielsen. 2016. Tree boosting with xgboost-why does xgboost win" every" machine learning competition? Master's thesis, NTNU.

Jayant Panwar and Radhika Mamidi. 2023. Panwarjayant at semeval-2023 task 10: Exploring the effectiveness of conventional machine learning techniques for online sexism detection. In *Proceedings of the 17th International Workshop on Semantic Evaluation (SemEval-2023)*, pages 1531–1536.

Barbara Plank, Dirk Hovy, and Anders Søgaard. 2014. Learning part-of-speech taggers with inter-annotator agreement loss. In *Proceedings of the 14th Conference of the European Chapter of the Association for Computational Linguistics*, pages 742–751.

Francisco Rodríguez-Sánchez, Jorge Carrillo-de Albornoz, and Laura Plaza. 2020. Automatic classification of sexism in social networks: An empirical study on twitter data. *IEEE Access*, 8:219563–219576.

Maximilian Schmidhuber and Udo Kruschwitz. 2024. Llm-based synthetic datasets: Applications and limitations in toxicity detection. *LREC-COLING 2024*, page 37.

Sebastien C Wong, Adam Gatt, Victor Stamatescu, and Mark D McDonnell. 2016. Understanding data augmentation for classification: when to warp? In *2016 international conference on digital image computing: techniques and applications (DICTA)*, pages 1–6. IEEE.

Michelle F Wright, Bridgette D Harper, and Sebastian Wachs. 2019. The associations between cyberbullying and callous-unemotional traits among adolescents: The moderating effect of online disinhibition. *Personality and individual differences*, 140:41–45.

Rayden Xu. 2022. Jigsaw rate severity of toxic comments. `https://www.kaggle.com/competitions/jigsaw-toxic-severity-rating/discussion/308938`. Last accessed on 2024-05-02.

Xiaogang Xu, Hengshuang Zhao, Vibhav Vineet, Ser-Nam Lim, and Antonio Torralba. 2022. Mtformer: Multi-task learning via transformer and cross-task reasoning. In *European Conference on Computer Vision*, pages 304–321. Springer.

Mengyuan Zhou. 2023. Pinganlifeinsurance at semeval-2023 task 10: using multi-task learning to better detect online sexism. In *Proceedings of the 17th International Workshop on Semantic Evaluation (SemEval-2023)*, pages 2188–2192.